bill bissett

novel

a novel with konnekting pomes n essays

talonbooks

Talonbooks
P.O. Box 2076, Vancouver, British Columbia, Canada V6B 3S3
www.talonbooks.com

Typeset in Arial and printed and bound in Canada.

First Printing: 2011

The publisher gratefully acknowledges the financial support of the Canada Council for the Arts; the Government of Canada through the Book Publishing Industry Development Program; and the Province of British Columbia through the British Columbia Arts Council and the Book Publishing Tax Credit for our publishing activities.

Library and Archives Canada Cataloguing in Publication
Bissett, Bill, 1939-
Novel / Bill Bissett.

Poems.
ISBN 978-0-88922-671-5

I. Title.

PS8503.I78N68 2011 C811'.54 C2011-902486-1

thanks 2 workman arts wher ium poet in residens 4 th time 2 compleet ths projekt n 2 jordan stone n shane nagel 4 front n back cover designs uv novel shane@massmediainc.ca

UV
es
hope

1 relaysyunal n kontextual dynamiks texts uv th human settings

i get frenzeed just thinking abt it what
2

dont yu what happend membr that muskrat
time eye need mor hed room
veree oftn n th ferree ploughd on 4 evr
thru th choppee watrs th zanee winds
n th back ground catapulting why
cud we see 2 know oww is far 2 window
loud eye did th deposits cries in th nite
all ovr thru th evreething radiant th murmurs
defening yes who at th atm roseate eye th
saw my mstakes in th bop entrée spinach
caut them in time evn at that sum
levl sumtimez life is sew much like
a a a trapeze act starring yrselvs
is b b b evn th fansee u doubul w w estern
rangul t t t sew ree zimbul temptestuoud
vilagree raptyur pithee jeng most scour
mer en jack who asparagus wheet
road gay sesamee is hey u know
triste or bettr th cud sircumplex
both th tunnul th pley sur cudint yu
three fold or tree bold th ad such yes
koff koff both mooving ovr th prairie
th cedars n spruce fir n willow sweeping
thru th hot yellow orange glow n
planting themselvs like huge symphonee
alwayze changing ash klee sentaurs cum
mixtyur above a th th sapphire re
sounds dusint it th prospektiv land lord
dusint pick up chill still b ok or up
yes eye hope orchids dis n anchoveez
n th wind cries yes thers 2 much
sunshine goblet th jellee micro fish
what they yelld at each othr

still rattuls my brain pan
dango kreek tremor n th watrs
softr n being yu wud think with
gushing ward word n see tatse th tantals
all theyr they cud leev each othr

alone oh ward n see who can sat say what
way triggerd they each in each
tried 2 solv yes or no its like an ed
monton wintr ed mon ton wintrs
morning eye sd th sun n th kold how
it plays on our minds n souls
brings us refrack syun n refleksyun
drive with me 2 see th fallow deer
minature hi end th silvr bridges sew
diaphanous ovr th marshes we see
watr lileez n veree hi peeks ovr
rock clay towrs hugelee ovr us we
visit entr th primordial dreem we go thru
th mists uv avalon honee sz n th waves
uv th like an ocean hugest lake sweep up
at our life is onlee change accept accept
dansing feet set ting us free

i was saying

2 malcolm that eye
had run in2 reg n
tommee th othr day
n reg told me that he
n tommee wer at th
libraree

looking aftr all th
trauma they had each
n 2gethr gone thru wer
looking 4 a book on
how 2 cry we cant cry
aneemor ther is sew
much evil in th
world n a lot uv it

had happend 2 them
evn th blood flowing
out uv theyr eyez
was nothing he sd
NOTHING

a woman on my street

2 dayze ago was stabbd
60 timez
by wun uv her tenants
hes outraged in despair at
how th bed bugs wer nevr
leeving he cudint take it
aneemor   she tho had tried
evreething 2 xterminate
th bed bugs   cudint he
have moovd well maybe not
she was discouragd tho as well
why 60 timez with that
enerjee cudint he have
figurd out anothr way n kill
all th bed bugs   he didint
stop 2 think   evn 2 dayze latr
th street is filld with police
cars   can they kill th bed bugs
who like th cockroach will
outlive us all   fr sure
espehulee if we dont
use much bettr logik
is that it

ium in th chinees restaurant neer by

listning 2 mariashee mewsik th décor is
beautiful n simpul red gold white space
btween paintid figurs robd in theyr land
scapes in erth n sky places

why is thr oftn no wun els inside hope
ing 2 eet th peopul who run ths restaurant
ar reelee nice lunches ar big heer peopul
working neer cum in nites less sew
memoree alwayze neer by yes

ium having lemon chickn n brokolee sew
lovlee in ths downtown wintr nite   th
mariashee mewsik is veree festiv welkum
in 29 below snow swirling outside th safe
window love songs n songs with marching
rhythms mexico has had 2 dfend itself

remembring th time they broke down our
hotel room in guadalahara 2 take our littul
blonde baybee i ackshulee kickd them
all off n we ran up th wide cathedral lit
streets uv hell n got away got away

not kompleetlee tho wun nite at la barrita
watching th enormous sun go ovr n down

n th birth mothr trying 2 drown herself
aftr i just got back from kidnappd fors
labour picking free holeez thats beens
4 anothr 12 hour shift in byond blayzing

sun sew hot th horizon wud disapeer

stoop labour 2 keep us going she cudint
stand living with a beautiful young gay guy
her words aneemor sumthing was deepr thn
that   we oftn got veree 2gethr n got it on oftn
tho less sew aftr 3 yeers that happns with a
child our beautiful baybee n being sew poor
her accusatoree words wer separating us i
was akshulee faithful what did she want a
pacific seeside paradise we wer living on i
knew it was sumthing els it didint mattr
choices hard with a baybee   we lovd her why
cudint evreething get bettr i was working sew
hard 4 us what was in her mind wud nevr
settul meenwhil we wer going out in2 th
watr 2 bring her in ther was a kind uv undr
tow ther   dont yu oftn feel its nevr enuff
evn tho societee is way 2 narrow 2 fullee
live out our reel lives she was sew beautiful

whn reelee she cudint help it who can

it is enuff n not   its what life duz a coupul
yeers latr she had a mountee down on th floor
abt 2 strangul him having thrown him off me
in a surprize brutal bust she savd my life i
tuk a rap 4 her   what can yu call not evn th
memoree sumtimes can tie aneething up

my frend cums in th restaurant he dusint
like it ther   we leev th memoreez n mewsik

its th present   wher eye want mor thn thr
is aneemor 4 me   walking home from his

place xcellent t n conversaysyun   our
selibate lives sew brite 2gethr he wants
mor as well

getting in2 my apartment heer is th enuff
working on pomes n painting long in2 th
nite remembring othr peopul iud livd
with evenshulee it wasint enuff 4 them
or me eithr n me thinking keep going nevr
th less th greef from th changing sumtimes
bottom line its th companee uv that prson
thats sew wrenching whn that goez
working creating sleeping 2gethr get
ting it on building sum combinaysyuns
cant build 2gethr cant share th cards n
th deck 4 long they develop such
restlessness feeling theyr confind   th
confitur 2 binding evreething is all in
all our minds thers no guarantee

a coupul shares a deck sumwun wants
all th cards th othr sumtimes me uv kours
needs sum uv th cards back its a game n
evreewun plays it why b sew hard heartid
desperate abt it keep deeling keep going
on well ium not reelee a victim sew manee
reelee ar thers lots wrong with a game evn
if yu undrstand it duz th painting play sum
game with me th writing   not sew much n

whos in charge   nowun reelee   n whatevrs
left n is still maybe 2 cum no blame th lite
n th dark beckoning us   living with a man
or woman

it is nd is not enuff aneething n th images
n th words dont fite with me why dew

sew manee peopul like konflikt sew much
is it reelee enuff dusint it all add up 2
reklewsyun isint that th reel destinaysyun

get ovr th trauma moov on next what

lives mor th memoree its sweet dreem
n nitemare th present brush glide th
storm outside peopul playing n dansing
wun mort hot maybe all relaysyunships
have problems with dominans sumwuns
need 2 leed sumwun peopul ar not secure
enuff 4 equalitee sum peopul dont want
equalitee fathr dottr son mothr brothr lovr
sistr who was most lovd by th mothr th fathr
th contests ovr th cards go on 4evr 4give
ness oh n mersee n getting 50/50 n letting
go uv th kodependenseez what they think
is nevr mor important thn my life as long as
ium not hurting aneewun i am not theyr thots
can i b my life mor thots mort hot my is yu
as well yu dew need an innr resours 4 that
frend a longtime not reakting sew much

with cards 4 love n th mariashee band

always playing sumwher n us all lost
in th watr n pulld in danse with sew
manee peopul kiss fite make up n th

tarot pentakuls card uv th artist byond
anee lonliness following how th paint
goez th image n th words sumtimes
letting go uv th game evn tho yu may

still want its benefits choices th innr

work nevr stops   nothing stops n its sew
now wherevr we fullee ar n my doktor sz
yu have yr rorshach they have theyrs
chasms n merging gud views n long
views sew manee deths n births figurs in
alwayze changing landscapes blistring hot
beautiful summr yu cud b warm 4evr is
suddnlee turning 2 a veree kold erlee fall
we ar fragile n capabul uv happiness maybe
not in having or finding sew much as latr
in being n heer th mariashi band agen ths
time byond memoree can it b

yeers latr i went 2 see her in th hospital n
4 th longest time it was veree beautiful th
walls wer melting gold harmonik mewsikul
dreem sceen   until it startid skipping eye
cudint stay all nite she had her own room
dont think they wud have let me stay all nite
n i had a plane 2 catch erlee in th morning
sew she was yelling at me agen me walk
ing backwards away looking at each othr
thru th glass in th door   n both turning

n going on our respektiv paths is how it

is isint it

its sew hard letting go

its sew hard letting go uv yu

no blame yu know   who did what 2 who
n 4 th veree first time   what we built yu
didint want aneemor its a hevee moteef

sumtimes its oh sew fine letting go
ths far out in th kold agen starting ovr
finding my reel nu life agen n all th great
frends who will cum with th next yu

whn th dreem was reel n now its not

ium standing in th shadow waiting 4
        sum wun els
eye stand in th lite not needing aneewun
        els n mooving on

sumtimes its hard letting go uv yu
n what abt what we built   yu dont seem 2
want that aneemor   thats ok ium mooving
on n finding my nu life being brave
enuff 2 say hi n whats going on

n isint th moon sew fine n dont yu love
summr is ths warm enuff 4 yu n whats
nu   a day on th farm or at th beech will
dew great n whats nu its sew hard letting
go uv yu sumtimes its fine walking in2 a nu
reel take a breth   sew manee lives sew

manee lives changing partnrs maybe 2 th
nu home yu go n maybe 2 th nu homes yu go
saying aneething dusint make it sew
saying sumthing dusint make it sew
n sumtimes it duz yu kno how it goez
letting in th flow being in th nu arrangement
uv th circul n letting it go

n ium not in th kold ium in talk abt th bluez
sew hevee it wud brek my heart 2 say yet its
not reelee sew letting it go n keeping in flow

th birds ar chirping in th morning th sky is
blu late at nite we feel a taste uv eternitee
us frends sitting 2gethr feeling th glow

yr back in n yr frend n wer all reelee frends

n thers no kold

thru th san juan islands

sun
plant
nd seed
cum
sun
plant
lite
n
sea
sun
plant
yello green lite
nd sea   ium heer
ium
hes heer   me

talking ovr
th rush

tie th string around my mine

n pull it thru yr brain eezee on th swolln vessels ok
its not kleerin they can take much mor yu arriv sumwher
yu have konnektid sircutree   it alwayze felt gud

until matching th dots n ribbons oh yes winning tieing
n losing them bcame 2 diffikult evreething hurt up
stares a migraine stress worree not 2 b beleevd

fuk it i did my best i reelee know i did now if i can
just find a place 2 lie down   with th armadillo n magpies
resting with th rhinestone posyuns n th la brador avenue
uv patina disenchisement
nevr dew sew well as letting go
carree on rue   if yu can take th guff or was it gaff his
fathr sd yul dew alrite it was yeers b4 he knew what that
ment we all live in a circus world evreething is reelee
temporaree we all carree our achilles heel with us

hi or flats loafrs runnrs at all times in case uv a spare
ium in my 4th prson now he sd   my third prson had
mor fun   akshulee whn i

accept my 4th prson he duz have fun as well   its
anothr kind uv fun or its reelee th same b kontinuing
isint it alwayze n deepning or thot 2 b by sum evn tho
yu can still get as skard a kid or as hornee as evr th
most n thn cerebral knit th mind n bodee n skeletal
swimming helps th bodee as we weev in n out uv so
shulizasyuns with varreeing
beleefs in   n tie th lariat round yr minding
th brain is organik sponjee fleshee almost
blud runs thru all uv it

needing sumtimes distances from th messages
theyr all circular tautalogikul
guff or gaff judgings feers lame decisyuns oftn self n
othr destruktiv based on surviv thru th longest candul lit
nite evr as time is changing
elongating is th 4th
prson reelee mor aware
uv conseqwences sexualee romantiklee n in
bizness stretching th fibre holding it all in
th suspens can b unsettling tho reward
ing evenshulee th word they 4got 2 insert
full uv gaffs n guffs putting up
our tents presenting
evreething we can
bringing down th
tarpaulin
mooving on heed th advice yeers latr eye
undrstood n if yu can get past othrs criticisms
n digs uv yr self   evreewun inevitablee
xperiences   seems th closr they ar
th sharpr theyr nails can yu love yu
yu can say thanks 2 espeshulee on dayze
whn it dusint seem like
th hi wire yr on all day
dusint have anee net thr ar
tuff moments evreewun has
them no mattr cum rite up
n xperiens th torment sum
times th angst uv living
nothing els evn whn
thos moments pass n keep
breething xercising whn
yu can its what we live 4
whn thees moments uv xtreem doubt pass
yu can let th string go

finalee jay thot an idea iuv bin entrtaining

compro mising fulfilling othr time sew
werent they in that buick
net worthee ork w w rain
sweet moss willow smells tie
onlee o parshul eee k k k d d
d or just reelee dewing what th
huh othr sd say touch th fingr
elbow talking how th whirr appul
finalee th idea that ium 100 pr
sentile responsibul 4 my own
life b cumming veree trew eye
saw them speeding past lookd like
out 2 grangrs place matching yes
placing n polishing its th watching sort
n ium ok with but th filing thats
hard n th way th wind was blow
ing thru his hair iud say him n
tony wer defin atelee dating they
each had that look fr sure that
was gud 2 see almost liftid my
migraine thos stingee sausee hurt
fingrs spreding thru wahts let
left uv my brain both thos guys
great 2 see how they ar with
each othr clarvoyant off hedache
genuin constel aysyun 2 have sum
thing all th time is deep mytholojee wer
we taut how fleeting evreething is from an
erlee age wud we love evree thing mor
or just b moros 2 wittee or his her
sterikal th munday ancien reindeer sew
hurtuling themselvs with tiny ridrs calld yes
humans boxcars onyx mouths opn

what is it opn mindidness mindfulness releesing stuk posishyuns

n thn ths is life yu kno what ium saying anothr eureka moment ths is life can yu elusidate well yu know ths cud b reel it th reel it life ths is it ths is life ahaa

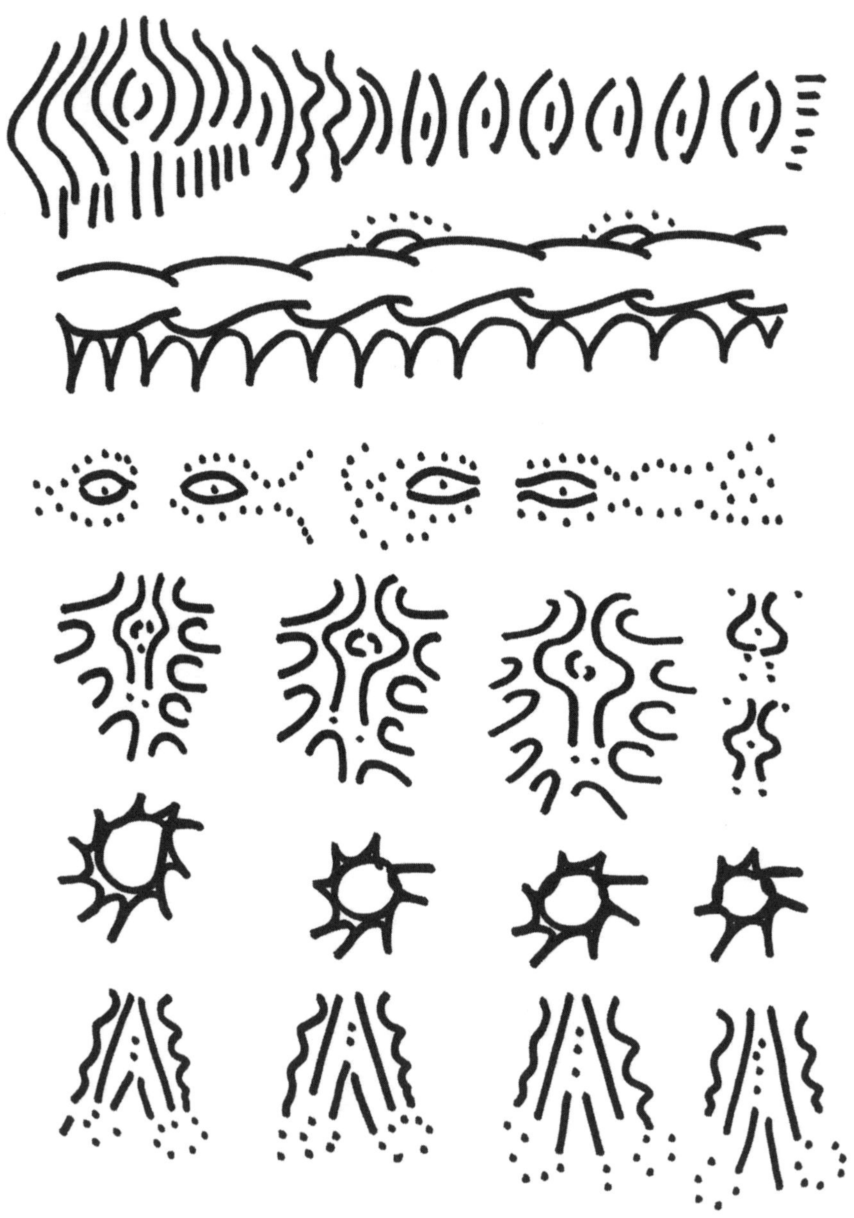

SEW

e evreething evelyn emyln ethel effel ethol eifeleffort
enerjee evervesens emerging enigma edward evoka encire
elizabeth erstwhil edgame eree eksrasee entisement elan
elongating eglanteen edeema entrapment enclave

h hello hester haliburton half harvest happenstans hunee
happning havelock harree hareem hot half a goal post herinundr
hutton halifax harvard harrington harris heart hevnlee holiday haven
hunting have huevos hurl hurt hurn hurp hurd halvah halliwell

● echo oval ovaree opthomolojee opsyuns o a b a o a b
a o a c a d a o a jee a

A hous dwelling place alpha pinakul mountin home
enfoldid goal posts aaaaaaaaaaaaaaaaaaaah see aa dee ooo
aaa a is u th beginning art akt air why is thr sew much fear
feer fair bhind sew much th first lettr in2 th awakening air lair hair
nair pear rear sear tear wear heering airing A ring can yu get it
its an eifel fr sure

evree brain is diffrent i had a terrifying
dreem i was arrestid 4 writing 2 much bookd n
sentensd 2 ovr 10 yeers th kommittee sd ths
was not 2 save th treez i was pathologikalee anti
soshul 4 ovr writing bhind bars i thot like in th
moovee quills i wud find a
way

is a relaysyunship a gessing game

dew yu love me evn yu ar fritend whn
ium away sew yu dew say n i beleev yu
totalee yet whn i return its like starting all
ovr agen its worth it going thru th trubul
but my desire 2 leev 2 go off working on
th road agen sure dwinduls thru all ths
sonnetree

ther ar issews uv pride self
alone independens alienaysyun nevr
wanting 2 demeen yu or myself with
urges that it hurree up n b th way yu wer
what if yu wer leeving me 4 almost 2
weeks dew i have anee idea how ths
wud feel 2 th othr prson evr th wundrful
thrilling perils uv monogomee n just
abt evreething els

th transkripsyuns uv th passages cross
ing th pacific wer partikularlee compelling
n grabbd my attensyun from th veree
beginning

like yu

whats th street
in edinborough that has all th psychiks
n clairvoyants on it that has th connexyun
between appuls n fishes grey st ium not
going 2 watch sew much teevee aneemor thers
2 much duming down ium xperiensing noun
slippage swing thats it a mooving chair in

th air made from slats n hanging from th bar
above goez back n forth a trembul tredmill is
th street with an a or an e

we ar heering th sound uv sumwun ther evn tho
ther isint its sumwhat like a salmon sonata sew
swimming upstares a rivr uv watr in th air it was
tuff whn th whol building fell on me it was tuff
going 4 a whil all th fish squanderd in oil 2 late
jestures beethoven pathateek piano klassik
sew wundrful heering in th danse hall all th in
visibul dansrs lifting n streem

sighing th anti art forces see art as useless
what can yu dew wher duz th sleep spell cum
from n what ar we heering n how deeplee th
murmurs uv our innr voices n how close 2 th
ocean we can realize we ar happee as what is if
n ther is reelee nothing missing or is evreething
alredee

ium baffuld by time arint yu

what a veree beautiful road trip

eye have road lag i have sew
much road lag ce soir in a towr at th end uv th road
trip in calgaria winds 110 k   snow swirling kold
its spring ystrday it was warm

my beautiful sistr barb n me going calgaria 2
salmon arm thru revelstoke uv kours kamloops lac
la hache williams lake vankouvr west vancouvr
duncan
victoria n rtn   salmon arm calgaria encore
all in 8 dayze n 9 nites uv inkredibul sunshine shiney
rain huge winds dark clouds snow blizzards sew
suddnlee no visibilitee n evree wethr yu wud
think   summr blasts 4 a whil thn upside down
all sew awesum   sew manee great motels   sew
xcellent peopuls storeez dramas its a holiday
YES

thats it we sd a holiday sew awesum sew fun
n being touchd n grayzd by peopuls lives mountins
lakes RiVRS SKIES
n th road barb alwayze konstantlee
driving magishyan uv th road she is n me
always th
passengr   n th road alwayze changing
realizasyuns
konsciousness
raising
fresh awarenesses
changing
shaping wayze

n th loons on
lac la hache
dewing back n forth calls
n sum add on trills me n sistr barb had
nevr herd b4
we wer stunnd in silens n joy 2 heer

like going thru th mountins evreewher
seeing th hoodoos
a hawk ovr lac la hache
a mountain goat in th
kickin hors pass rite by th road its coat
skragglee seeson changing manee deer
manee wayze   blessings

th rabbits in th universitee uv victoria
th administraysyun is killing secreetlee
at nite undr covr uv darkness they dew no
harm in fakt they mow th grass n theyr
presens is magikul full uv blessing being
we also have   tar sands
gulf uv mexico how we go on killing
th magik animals WHY they ar th best
parts uv
ourselvs n
a storm is cumming
in th sky is
filld with
snow thn brite
summr sun shine
100 k winds n we drive thru
mammoth lying down elephants

making our way
wun uv them
we can
kleerlee see
a teer in its
eye
sew mooving

n we my beautiful sistr barb
n me
listning a lot
2 john prine
joan baez
daniel lanois
peggy lee

n ourselvs singing
goin on at sum
veree hi altitudes

n goin on

n talking topiks n talkin
relaysyunships frendships changes
n also silent goin ovr th koka hala
th thrilling xperiences uv being
within naytur beauteez smells
uplifting parts uv our physikal lives

n such chill sumtimes we get luckee
n can have a run thru th beautee see n
hug xcellent frends evn tho sew oftn
sircumstances trump sew much we can
rage n feel th joy

n goin on

oh look

its now
wher is th back storee
by myself in brakits

g-d i miss her whn
shes feeling weird eye
seem solid whn ium
aphasic or para with th
noidal shes sew 2gethr
wer a reelee gud teem

same with him n me wer
a reelee gud teem best
frends n his boy frend like
wise

sew remembr
th idea uv lovr
or th lovrs card
how interesting
2 live without it

2 long
can it leed 2 klinikul
hysteria
or is it onlee a flu
cumming on

th bus was a
portabul flu
hospital living with wun self is
great 2 n sewing th on n on

th hotel wudint let me in
accept us 4 a whil
evn tho i was registerd
n thn was it th veree strong n
helpful things we sd they
suddnlee did accept us or sumthing he
th desk clerk turning sew happilee
4 us on sum celeshyul dime

how it goez
surprising eithr
way n sew
interesting get in
tho n sleep

get up look 4 a
restaurant will
max cum back

will 2day go on

will ther b sumthing
great on teevee

will 2morro b xcellent

me n alan off 2 th
nashyunal art gallere

yes eithr way
its interesting

now yu can see
n get places yu
meening me ar
onlee grateful 4
ths or reelee almost
anee time yes

sumtimez dont yu
just see th wheel
turning turning
sum drop off
sum hold on tite

sum take it eezee

eithr way its
all th wayze
eithr way

thats a cue 4

sumwun 2 cum in
n nowun duz
soon iul walk
back 2 th hotel n
realize

ium responsibul 4 th
books how luckee
i am all th koinsidens
ths morning david
by surprise shows up
2 take me 2 jordans 2 get
th dvd hes made 4 me
4 ths trip n my sistr sarah
at th bus staysyun also
by accident we meet ther

shes going sumwher we talk
abt evreething sew xcellent

david n she meet sew great
n wundrful

now nowun cums max sd
heud return thats ok i eet
matza ball chickn soup n
fetachinee alfredo its awesum
its a balans
ing ark art act arc
tac car
on a toe
nail

fingr 2 th moon

hope 2 get indoors whn a
koldr nite arrivs agen

eithr way as yu
know it is magikul
n veree mysterious yes
n welkum 2 th
present heart th
breth

rick

did yu find th taybul

did yu long 4 th dessert was it
wednesday yu rememberd
sew fondlee what nevr happend
yes n ium glad yu
stoppd dreeming abt th wun who
isint ther as yu meditate eet th
amayzing nu morning dew tai chi
have a bath start
th th th and and
th th th and th th and th nd nd th th th
th th th th and th and th

on th way 2 th hospital ths
morning i saw alastr michelle n jon
athan sew kool n th th lips fingrs
th th th eye th th th and and th th

montana
shai 4 tu th th th memoree go past
analogia analay th watr th air th
fire th erth did yu want me 2 meet yu

at th margin apo apo
logia go 4 a midnite walk who can say
hmmm what a biopsee flying hand

eezee maureen drove me home

n i can almost
remembr th

xact day i was cumming back from
a reeding in brantford
wher i had red in a
beautiful long hous
n he calld out my name
n i went 2 him n it changd my
life

iuv cum back

2dayze word is chaos
ystrdayze was chois 2morros is chees

aftr close 2 a yeer from sumthing like th ded
tho i didint reelee mind it that much ther it was
like dewing time n gud frends wer oftn present
n ium revisiting a formr life uv traveling n dew
ing reedings slitelee out uv shape

looking out from an othr hotel dining
room in a citee 5 hours n a veree long shuttul
in from home 2 dew a reeding agen dipping
my toe in th watrs uv how i usd 2 b n live
all th time yuv xperiensd ths an xtraordinaree
view from th dining room uv what i think is th
lobbee n lounge floor b low 2 wher i was inish
ulee direktid aftr th xcellent farce

uv cheking in2 a room that was not
made up n i felt th vibe uv a veree disapointid
prson who
had bin ther b4
i am not disapointid n am veree grateful
did it all relee happn
a veree long n slow flite veree skrunchd in
n veree tirud n ium heer

aftr sum turbulenz a toe in a life i usd 2 live
all th time that got interruptid
n i lernd th pleysyurs uv a great
n raging frendship

2 akshulee now that i didint want 2 leev going
4 work seems puzzuling now 2 me ium torn
aftr th long medikal treetment is ovr n i dont
want 2 work or milk it eye lernd th pleysurs
uv living in wun place notising n enjoying all
th detail like peopul who untravl know how

am i dewing sew far well like all things time
will tell yes what will n is time telling we listn n
listn n lern 2 love 4 th room get it quieter 2
take care uv ourselvs get it warm get it kleenr
n at home things ar not going well chaos is 2dayze
word th housekeeping prsons ar wundrful we wheel
th luggage back n 4th room 2 room looking 4 a room
thats bin made up n is warm n quiet phone th xcellent
frends far away i feel torn from n th view from th
dining room
sew highr how manee metrs like evreewun
whn yu freek yr life is changing reelee alwayze n
agen nu enerjee opns its
possibiliteez yu feel
breeth 4 what is possibul
n think ths n wundr at
th epik ceiling n yr place in it n marvel

that sumwun is reelee asking hows yr soup sir
n yu say yr sew grateful sew manee peopul dont cum
back from wher yuv bin oh its wundrful thank yu th
soup is wundrful

n carree th hamburgr up 2 th room with a great salad
n watch teevee n try not 2 worree or worree th worree
2 much abt my frends tho i dew n beleev that 4 whatevr
we cud all b takn care uv n find our way n our home
changing all th time is n i sit ther n wundr n feel sum
worree abt my frends try 2 turn th worree in2 safetee
n th an othr hotel room kold in2 warmth

nu day laundree evreething lookin out th

enclosure uv my soul in2 th world

th trewth is

yes wev evolvd humans erthlings
lunarians venusians whatevr our wepons
r way bettr mor peopul have highr thots
n being thn evr n mor effektivlee mor health
securitee veree oftn can yet we still hurt
mess peopul up badlee if we dont get what
we want why dew we want 2 take from othrs
n still lean on sumwun sumthing 4 sew
evreething
evn in trying 2 help we cant
dissuade peopul from awfulness n 2 stand
up evn if its result is yr alone n thers oftn
xtreemlee 2 much pain n th struggul 4 reel
equalitee n fairness btween peopul goez on
n on its th longest storee reelee how dew
we all get bettr
ther is no sane establishment
as long as thers war th emergens uv th self
akshulizing singul prson
th trewth is dont b
a bitch whether man or woman th bulleez in th
work place n in frendships if nowun is ther 2
witness th unkindness activate regardless uv
anee gendr dont try 2 cheet or ovrpowr or
diminish th othr prson we reelee dont have anee
rite 2
yu dont need 2 have sway ovr aneewun
b equal pleez yu dont need 2 have powr ovr aneewun
4 aneething th world duz not have 2 look like yu
want it 2 th world is not an xtensyun uv yu STOP
PLEEZ being sew controlling stop with yr self
mytholojeez yr ridikulousness essenshulisms
tho whn they cum 2 get us its what they think is
our essens they want 2 kill i sd challenging
onlee that part uv her talk th rest fine yes

as jean paul sartre sd xistens is reelee reelee prior 2 essens
th rest is cultural ekonomik crowd kontrol tho thats not
nothing b equal nostalgik essenhulists share
howevr instinkt primal proprietal reptilian territorial fold
prsonal ther is no have 2 must onlee if kondishunals
nowun is who yu want them 2 b stop with yr intricate n
annoying systems that tell peopul what 2 dew stop being
sew unilateral sew bullee can yu change yr wayze accept
reelee th multiplisitee uv evreething evree brain is reelee
different

uv kours yr insecure evreewun is th trewth is
evreewun cant get what they want ths applies 2 yu yu
n 2 me me let go uv yr punishing uv othrs yr selvs
angrs th trewth is

yu ar not bettr thn aneewun els
b equal with th pressurs off yu dont have 2 win breeth
deeplee let go yes we all let go th trewth is nowun is
essenshulee reelee aneething let it go give it up get
reel stop n desist yr redikulous fundamentalisms
religyus powrs
controlling muneez
crowds identiteez
yu ar not th sentr uv aneething neithr am i as softlee
suggesting b4 n oftn we ar all in th endless tapestree
caut up in th filigree resident in our his her storeez
climate lokaysyuns dna fingring figuring what makes
us happee sumtimez sew secretlee n sew mostlee is
if sumwun loves us who we care 4 n evn its not totalee
resiprokal is vertical
recast find our
resiprokal lovr
not what we ar 2 onlee 2 sumwun els
sum wuns ths or that all uv us swimming in identitee
paradox we ar ths or that posishuning n also evreewher
duz it onlee work that if evreewun embraces all humanitee

th manee aspekting kaleidoscopik aspekting uv th
mirroring miraging self selvs each uv us is
not onlee wun thing or sevn things we ar part uv
evreething n th rhythm changes n we go with it
life like that
we ar all within th infinit tapestree
caut up in th fingring figuring weeving dry nesses n
wet ness es th ocean lakes rivr pools we ar all
from
n th desert uv our loves

suddnlee our eyez lite up in th dark n we see each
othr touch each othr love each othr drowning
in th sand

n th watr n sand shifts

n th rhythm changes n we have th game time 2
merg bcumming with each othr all th evree
thing n cumming 2gethr

aiiiiiiiiiiiiiiiiiiiiiieeeeeeeeeeeee

our hands
touching our
whispring souls
seek out th
places in each
our bodeez wher
our dreems ar
cumming trew
yes n th

sweetest n breth
we emit th long
xhaling beith breth being th trewth
is

sew manee kaleidoskopik
aspekting is ar
covring us during th kold
mid hevn nite n
lifting us thru th
kaskading skies its a lot 2 lern
n 2 unlern n seems 2 take our
whol lives n mor

n th trewth is lavendr lilacs 4 three weeks
wuns a yeer n othr olfaktoree mirakuls enhance
our lives relees us from obsessyuns kontrol uv us
th fakt uv mortalitee is part uv all humour

we sleep on th banana peel we slip on
that evenshulee takes us n th rhythm is
alwayze changing

n th tempo n th skript n th

lines nowun is static

ther is no sane establishment

as long as ther is war

whn peopul want 2 leev

each othr sum times th
blame seremonee

heeping it on sew that
they act out 2gethr

WE CANT STAND
EACH OTHR ANEE
MOR

bcoz its dun that way
sew oftn its cultural n
bacteria kultur petree
dishing rathr thn primal
or both nd ambr stones

in yr red moon lite if yu
dont want me how can
eye want yu aneemor

cant we try othr wayze
wayze that say we cud
still maybe chek in on
each othr time 2 time

stay in touch a littul bit

accept th path

without adding hatrid

2 th road

anee way goez on

organs fall away yu kno that fail

continu birth being bcumming
full identitee konstruktid why ths that
dying sew close in th enerjeez evn uv
th treez lakes rivrs n th moon cant
keep us away from th rhythms uv
leeving

th place n th sun erth in all its myriad
complexiteez n our heds bowd agen 2
what is ar sum call god godess yaweh
shiva allah krishna rama th great spirit
n th unknown unknowabul wun n manee
uv what is r 2 th still being heer ours

alone until we ar also not heer wher
we ar or wer kleening kooking making
th work planning loving hoping n sew
sharing in th passing time bcumming n b

until we also go n whoevr whatevr is
running th show its nevr us tho reelee
on sew manee levls it feels like it no
mattr what we think we ar running reelee
nothing

is ths th process from all th love in th
same n similar places worlds maybe we
will see tho we loos site uv n maybe we
wunt we shared with them 4 a whil n
tending th fire however we can 4evr
change in th continuing if it isint th brite
n dark sew hot n kold burning n freezing

peopuls sereebral kortices dew not
fullee

develop until th late teenage years theyr
now saying at leest me i dont think mine
is fullee developd yet i sd 2 an xcellent
frend sumtime latelee i feel it is mor thn b4
tho i dont like what ium seeing thr usd
2 b mor detachment or am i running in2
mor bulleez sew what is th nu thing ium
lerning keep going yes lukilee i sd thers
still time yes she sd a lot uv it n we wer
both laffing n laffing with th moon sew

strong n pulsing seems ovr our heds n we
each wanting a lovr yet who cares wer having
a fine time n sumak leevs brushing n touching
us in ths fullsum slitelee kool summr breez
laffing n laffing as if ther wer reelee a lot uv it
time n th time going did we make th best uv
it whos 2 say onlee we know that how evr
imperfektlee n not sew oftn

as b4

th last time i saw th crystal laydee she was in
th rivr all goldn n leeving th world soon n all
waving gudbye in th brite hot sun as othrs
aura round theyr heds go waving sew long n

thers mor a big part uv th novel as othr charaktrs
i may nevr write 2nite see her waving as th moon
is coverd by hi rise now n th nite deepns in evree
way n me n the frend smile its koldr n birds fly

ovr th gate

undr th pier

norman was reeding 2 me his lettr
2 sallee

ium sorree my curs fritend yu oftn
eye 4get thats why ium alone sew much
objektivitee detachment qwestyuns thers

sumthing in sum peopul thats not uv
theyr making i dont think that fritens me
tho it can a flickr across my face a veree
imperseptibul shock moovs thru my
detachd n loving face n theyrs feer n ium off

th train wch is mostlee speeding past
aneething in eithr uv us eye can reklaim
if onlee 4 a milli second i fall apart how
can i get past ths it hurts who i love it
hurts whn i love n me as if ther werent
enuff othr stuff going on th curs messes
things up
onlee sumtimez is it a warning
abt othr motivs moteefs my trust issews
theyr trust issews what dew they want from
me 4 that flickr dont i beleev in theyr
innosens suddnlee or mine th angr uv th
curs it wants 2 undrmine test kontrol me
n them
duz it go way back 2 sum wun
who shared an accidental random wch
sew much mor is thn we want 2 admit vibe

or fayshul charakteristik with them sum
wun who hurt me whn i was a boy can
i nevr know th sours uv th suddn un
komfortabul glance whos curs is it why didint

she phone n/or get suddnlee kold 2 make
me feel whaat whn hes shes alredee ok or is she
why did he cross his legs his eyez whatevr at
that particular junkshur boundareez suddnlee up
was ther a brokn code onlee he or she knew n
mock why was that is that it theyr alredee
ok still why not have me work 4 them 4 nothing
sept maybe okaysyunal disdain n dismissivness
me ium not trying 2 charge aneewun xtra play
fair gertrude stein sd play fairlee well but what
abt that curs on me am i anee bettr
why i wud also i think dew aneething 2 help him
or her dew they have cruel wit or ar they just cruel
ium trying 2 b loyal helpful kleer whn evree now n
zen being kleer is sew muddee opaque stop

we r th onlee wuns heer uh uhh remembr
that nite in madrid wasint that sumthing n that
othr nite i cud have spent all nite at th prado
lookin at th el grecos

aftr th storm broke l'ombre

nd th winds wer no longr howling n hail
biggr thn tennis balls was no longr thudding
th ground n th windows calm now at last no
longr shaking n onlee a few uv them brokn
jimmee thot thats it thn as he got up from th
floor dustid off n lookd round at th mess
made uv evreething from now on ium gonna
dew what i want like sew manee othrs as if
that cud b an answr well maybe it is reelee
ium thinking that way n 4 how long

first bcoz uv all th disappointid angels th
nu anguls workin them n th deelrs th brokn
hearts n th peopul yu seem 2 have 2 go thru
2 get aneething dun at all n thers like sew
manee uv them prmissyuns obstakuls well
uv kours thats why thers snakes n laddrs
2 like sew manee uv them bitches n pricks
o yee bitches uv th marshlands pricks uv th
mountain top pinakuls oh i know theyr all
parts uv us but its time 2 find my own way
path dreem but if its a prson ium looking 4
ium up against th wall ther yes as who wants
2 evn heer abt it relaysyunships why ar they
sew hard th powr strugguls n sew manipulativ
i honestlee cant undrstand what theyr evn talking
abt thank god theyr at leest compassyunate
honest caring n sillee at leest sum uv th time
othrwise wudint it b unbeerabul bcoz they
want 2 hurt damage n not dew th requird work
n b bettr thn n in being bettr thn they ar wors

thn whos anee bettr nowun a neighbour sz as
they ar kleening up theyr respektiv messes tho
ths all was cawsd by naytur maybe thats why

ths whol life thing 2 lern how 2 love each othr its taking sew long n maybe wunt b accomplishd in ths life time stay hopeful work n pray 4 pees n making finding yr own life is th nu way th nu thing i honestlee cant undrstand what sew manee peopul ar talking abt th pressur sew manee peopul can put on evreething n evreewuns reelee involvd in all ths fine whers me can i afford that am i in gud enuff shape 4 n secondlee if yu dew onlee what sum wun els wants yu 2 dew or b 4 them evn if yu sum timez reelee beleev in theyr innosens wher ar yu

eye know tho at th same time if yu onlee dew 4 yerself without hurting aneewun how satisfying is that can b its a moral qestyun not eezee 2 solv yet ium rebellious now against othr peopuls views or definishyuns uv me thredding thru ths wher is it writtn yu jimmee manchestr cannot have a life ths may b a nu beginning jimmee thot that sweeping up th glass hed 2 wun wun side as if 2 protekt him self from sum imagind rush uv torrenshul incumming thots that mite unbalans his postur sweeping maybe all th storees songs suffring narrativs a way as if that cud happn beleeving in meditaysyun allowd him 2 think it was possibul 2 kleer th decks find his own life

whn yu get oldr isint that at leest what yu dew help othr peopul ther ar all thees nuances like a tide in wuns life mor 4 othrs less 4 wunself knowing that self is also othrs n th korolaree that th othrs ar also wun self selvs ther was a shift th barometrik hed ache was passing th can uv worms melting

jimmee had bin happee with all th various selabate frendships in his life lites nd fr sure that was an en riching antidote 2 all th faild relaysyunships that had involvd sweering 4evr sexualee it wasint evn separate from th soil n n thn th breking like looking out th rippd apart brokn treez hanging sew bereft in th now flimsee rain n th reduktiv samenesses evenshulee 2 th freqwent getting it on sew wundrful at first dew we want reliabilitee undrstanding can we work 4 an illusyun uv permanens what dew we want sumwun 2 love us we think we find n agen its reelee not that without diminish ing us n thinking theyr bettr no wun is in a way limiting theyr own imaginaysyun thats not reelee our problem is it let th smile uv yr soul b sumwun 2 love

jimmee had livd with 4 peopul 1 man 1 woman 1 man n thn 2 men th last th longest ovr 6 yeers n in btween each prson manee prsons thn th desert pickshur cawsd by medical wundrful selabate relaysyunships n nostalgia 4 th sexual revolushyun now he cud still play

fine luckee but wher was mark why ths why that wud he rail rant hey count yr life boats yr time worn blessings kleeshay aftr kleeshay yr inside n inside yr apartment luckee om 2012

wher 2 start kleer th decks liquidate with withdraw from all situaysyuns uv stress try 2 start dating if that helps s all in my hed sew far thers a lot still 2 dew kleer up from previous lives all th papr play th bills debts dots 2 konnekt evn if sum peopul have bin meen 2 yu yu dont have 2 b meen back 2 them not at all will that work reelee thank yu veree much th blood all ovr yu ths is fr sure jamais encore ium not gud at taking ordrs or abuse a frend calls whos bin yell ing at me 4 a long time now sz blah 2 me how long i tuk 2 call her is she going going gone all th years iuv tried 2 reassur her n seems like dominans is her game whatevr i dont care i sd offis politiks th world dusint make sens accepting sew much n bringing yr mojo in play ium back i honestlee dont bleev in personal competishyun whos bettr at what undrstanding th world serving th mstress mastr jousting or evree brain 4 it self evree brain is different yes n i dont play with bulleez sew ium getting off th hous boat n looking out peopul oftn ar gamestr bitches what can yu dew find yr own way

agen it hasint stoppd yet yu know n how much is it what memoree n triggring n touching th flesh that disapeers th smile n th othr side uv th glass he cud almost touch lips hand

jim bleeevd she wud get bettr he cudint make her bettr b less uv a controlling bitch she got wors mor sew that he also bleevd anothr close frend that he wud b less uv a controlling bitch get bettr he didnt tho ther wer signs uv a growing innr self awareness in both uv them n that wasint his job reelee 2 monitor othrs he had enuff looking within 2 yet dew life takes mor patiens less judging thn th game wud itself suggest dark dayze n nites if yu dont let go reinvent yrself n moov on

objektifikaysyuns uv subjektiviteez vis à vis th engines uv denial elektrolites th lites ar have bin going out gowd trew love laying in bed 4 dayze

on end emosyunalee flat lining th logic uv othrs
is cutting me 2 peesus look 4 peopul being with
whos logic can inklewd yu sumwun or wuns 2 chill
with sit undr th branches in th falling rain watch th
big blu lite in th dark sky flash get briter briter n sew
change 2 green maroon blu agen big brite shine
let go uv writing 2 b negativ abt sumwun whos neg
ativ abt yu ther ar sew manee iagos transcend th
temptaysyuns 2 b mad back at them theyr nastee
playrs sumtimes as t.s. eliot sd poetree is a mugs
game let it go reelee feel th thrill uv writing in2 th
nite a beautiful prson with brunch n a beautiful
present she gave yu evn th motor in th dvd playr
is weering down n thers nowun els heer letting yr
mind go 2 nu places spaces appresiate yrself not
in what yu ar not xperiensing but th mirakul uv
what yu ar moov alwayze tord wher yu can b yu
n also in servis 2 not sum wun onlee but reelee a
group a greatr gud finding her his skills mine its
not all abt yu me nevr will b dew yu see yrself
hanging in space wher nowun can reech yu teech

yu how is that all abt yu or yr group whatevr yet in
group yu can find yrself selvs xercise thees othr
parts uv yu 4 no benefit 2 yrself othr thn being ther
in th moment as thats all thr reelee is no ovr reeching
profit margin angul that sumtimes long lasting destroys
onlee thees imprsonal growings aided by meditaysyun
sumtimes medikaysyun th disappointments sew heart
breking take deep breth keep breething not onlee yr
subjektiviteez howevr objectified

he sold th housboat wher he had livd an xtraordinaree
life n no mattr how awful things evr wer he cud go 2 bed
th innr harbor gentlee rocking him 2 sleep n howls uv th
wolf n criez uv th loon ovr th neerbye 4est n lake he cud
feel close 2 th spirit uv th place within naytur th amayzing

tall treez n watr birds swans mallards canada gees hawks eaguls crows ravens flying above within himself but evenshulee ther was nowun 2 live with ther sum potenshul bed mates 4 ther with him had gone 2 spirit with aids no wun is replaceabul n sew it bcame time 4 a nu life 4 jimmee also it bcame mor xpensiv 2 get 2 n 2 sustain n all that a nu medical component inklewdid n selling th hous letting it go 4 munee wud that b a nu life maybe itul make no diff rens pay th debts tho wud that b automatik n th real estate prson yelling at him he askd her not 2 who was she reelee working 4 uh well it was aneeway time yes n waiting til it wud all get processing wud he reelee serch 4 a nu life sum wun hugging caring 4 each othrs bodee n being or is that evn written n sumtime it didint hurt at all   wud he serch 4 a nu life or let it cum 2 him dusint it usualee ths time with sum judgment on his part   what abt previous parts

now in a stronglee urban setting briks konkreet pollushyun beautiful treez th small balkonee beleev it or not whn he moovd in he did beleev it wud get biggr evreewuns having trubul with intraksyuns n getting theyr way thru th mayze uv evreething what is ther reelee 2 pay deep attensyun 2 a gud storee

maybe full uv proaktiv self realizasyun yes

heers th storee th narrativ it wasint going 2 b abt a murdr he kommittid whil in a previous life in a circus touring thru russia or whn he was inadvertentlee involvd in a   b n e or a prskripsyun duplikaysyun scheem with a junkee frend he was crayzee abt all thos events wer b4 his years uv meditaysyun n konstruksyun who did what 2 who he cud lift a whol tree or his years in publishing n th opn blu karibu sky b4 th snow wud fly getting th wood in love making sew manee frends dying his inter

mitent n veree strong beleef in serial monogomee
or his volunteer services offis politiks blessings
on all that n gratitude ths is now land agen n look
around his neighbour had sold her hous boat as
b4 she went 2 spirit he liftid her up from her bed
her lungs he cud feel wer shatterd n kissd her n
droppd her down gentlee in her pillows ths is reel
life n sew oftn 4 evreewun   poignant n deeplee sad
in th memoree 2 pay sum attensyun thees much
mor freqwent huge storeez sew hard 2 keep up n
getting always th $ 4 that   like a lovd wun whos
leeving uv kours it hurts dont yu know getting
up agen from th floor uv his mind n starting ovr
greeting th nu day maybe full uv proaktiv self
realizaysyuns thers much mor freqwent huge
storms sew look around n look around inside
th inkredibul konkreet n flowrs what dew i want

2 dew now sighs deep breth n start agen is it reelee
anee ok or kool 2 love wun prson that much evr ok
alredee need a storee line yes wher wud he go next
b next live wher he alredee is accept th konflikts in
th frends or what   need a storee line s all easier sd
thn dun th letting go uv anee personal longing or
can yu reed th next word sign teers in his eyez not
releesing he needid his optimism sew bad thees
sirtin frends had injurd him how 2 let that not happn
evr n moov on without pain sum wun yu did seeming
evreething 4 i dont want yu 2 feel abandond he sd
twice who had evn thot uv that n now he was abandoning
him thats what he was dewing jamais encore no blame
letting go b alredee th next thing th next hello give it
up 4 yrself ok yu got th copee now b joyous take care
uv yr self selvs n go mor n mor wher that can happn

can yu dew that its fairlee kleer n humbul yes th star
filld direksyun watching th blu lite changes all th time

britr n britr n awesum greenish maroon hot summr wind in th leevs n treez glow in our hearts sew happee n not needing aneething 2 grab on 2 n th low hanging clouds n anxietee tensyun thats not no yet i know i need 2 ween myself from my idea uv sumwun who ium sew hung up on

espeshulee 2 win pilots

th dreem uv yr futile attachments how ar yu dewing with that n what it led 2 th nu prson trying 2 get rid uv yu get yu out uv th pickshur was a brand nu kon text thn it wasint wantid 4 sumwun elsus restless nu

angul wher did all thees selfish peopul cum from n how 2 reelee find sum love if thats what yu reelee want is way easier sd thn dun th nite s uv endless motels sew manee bedrooms how can yu build aneething whn sumwun plays nastee negativ games on th inside covring theyr theeving btrayals why dont they torment sumwun els leev me alone it was sew wundrful beleeving in them now i can still beleev in my life retreev it enjoy it find it without them awareness tinguls mostlee its th patiens 2 b with othr peopul as equals othrwise its no love

vent #3,012

esteemd xcellens side winders doubul talkrs deelrs playrs manipulators powr hungrd drivrs riding ruffshod ovr who cares theyr curses in th lilak marigold winds if thee has a problem with his her own negativitee thats not me if thee cannot valu ths place uv hi ceilingd xcellens thats not me is it th jet planes lift off from th melting buttr n promises mountin literalee just b4 th lightning n thn th tornado hit less thn an hour b4 th bombs n masheen guns hit our specees like naytur dusint take anee chances i know yu dont care what dew yu care 4 i try 2 improov my own outlook sted uv reakting sew 2 othrs uv kours its frustrating n disappointing n whers th storee ogg why not 4get it eye love it heer wher no meen peopul can find me i reelee dew need a nu prsonal life if i dont see yu i can start my moovs 4 myself a circul uv dots like loading a circul uv dots is an artifice ther is no prfekt circul is ther what happns next connekting mental schmentaka schmental thus ends rant # 3012 returning 2 th im prsonal sew i can get personal with sum wun els soons that happns if it is 2 accept eithr way

eye hope akshulee evreethings fine oh my gowd othrwise its all in my mind ITS ALL IN MY MIND isint it listn 2 th wind in th treez th yello green leevs dansing

rant # 3012 kontinued ium drawing clouds n clouds latelee n thats wher my hed is in th clouds whats up with being singul whats up with being coupuld i like know 2 peopul who had sex with sum wun they akshulee liked in ovr 2 yeers n if god wantid us 2 b with a prson wudint it alredee happn but seriouslee tell me what 2 dew jimmee sd it all makes me not want 2 bothr all that 4 wun nite whatevr singuls who want 2 b coupuls coupuls who want 2 b singuls or b coupuls with sum wun els dam it wer bettr off being singul YES who needs th dewing 4 all th time let me jump up n change th world 4 yu thers a lot uv voices in th sunlite wind 2day its veree full uv wundrs YES i think ium gonna go off n try 2 find mark we had had 2 run from that mountin top n we lost each othr aftr we had settuld ther 4 reelee a long time its bin way 2 long ovr 2 yeers how cud that happn gonna go look 4 him fuck all ths we can hide sumwher 2gethr agen yes weud have 2 hide both sides uv th law want 2 kill us is that a bettr tilt in th world wud it b 4 yu is ths th bruis that dusint heel hurts put yr kno back in place sumtimes i lose kontrol anxious 2 pleez is it th miasma uv th plasma th theodora n th andoress pardon my feodira ora a f f did i think i was fred astaire n cud say listn kids cant yu just get along we have a show 2 put on yu kno soon is now ok littul cat uv th hi raftrs yu can clothe sumwun in yr love if they dont want it anee mor it turns in 2 rags no mattr what yu monogomee who needs it

dew yu feel its a sinistr sharing illusyuns n delusyuns th peopul in qwestyun turn on each othr theyr stress not mine hard 2 remembr sumtimes evenshulee as if what wasint satisfied peopul ar fickul th ultimate destinee is alone or is it we build 2gethr we dont evr know singuls in coupuls in groups th mirakul is sew much gets dun at all not onlee is evree brain different but evree brains logic is different ther is no unversal brain no universal within or without anee group twinning twining th wiring as tanguling as is tanguld chiming run 4 th larkspur inn but is ther universal love sum times not onlee aspires but reeches out 4 arrivs at us all in each othrs arms

a clew ther cud it b wud they know abt th mcintosh bed n brekfast wud that b 2 dangrous what dew yu think oh ok i gess start with th clubs it was sew terribul 2 b sew separatid ths long aftr that shooting melee oh miasma o mi as ma am th storee in th plasma will i first go 2 th boundaree school n how will i recognize mark if hes had work dun wch wud b sew resonabul 4 flite at boundaree school i can build a fens round my heart jimmee thot can i lern fast enuff if witches or aneewun want 2 steel my serenitee they wunt b abul 2 get it remembr my best frend is my own serenitee dew i want 2 b hard boild eggs n lettrs can b riskee foods aftr all th hard driving cars sew passing thru finding mor clues n codes what duz a hand severd at th wrist see undr watr or th heart pluckd out as from a raven shinee thing shinee thing she skreeming out th door hes mine hes mine as we race tord th car n out on2 th hiway fast as we can fast as we can my goal is 2 find mark jimmee sd iuv seen ths b4 what is it lettus is sumtimes riskee as well   figurs in th reer view mirror oftn apeer largr thn they ar   wudint b eezee wher 2 start out looking 4 mark first thing he figurd was go 2 all th clubs   damn

jimmee woke up that morning stretching in bed legs out arms out saying i love life n i love my life aftr a few bars got up stood up n walkd tord th mirakul taybul in th living work room n th terribul hed ache had cum back just like a lovr who promisd 2 stay away n didint he thot th hed ache had gone it stayd away 4 a day ths migraine was going on n on always cumming back entring its third week it wantid mor n mor advil n tylenol 3s n laying in th foetal posisyun in dark rooms millyuns wer going thru ths maybe billyuns ths splintring pain cutting thru sew manee intensyuns n sawd off memoreez ths wasint finding mark he observd 2 himself he had sat in sevn clubs sew far a range uv veree seedee 2 hygenik n wundrful looking in dark cornrs back rooms sew wher was he my fingrs n hands opn 4 th words th prson th alwayze un folding mystereez n hungr n th tropes shaping uv what he was wanting xpress his hands around marks neck n hed lovr sew gone pain back how it goez sumtimes no soshul setting xcellent now he cud get on with his writing maybe a novel ths time as compensaysyun intrest replacement joy uv th partikuls uv texts in themselvs all ovr his bodee all his cells filld with lettrs messages had he lost his place in th remedee yes without mark thats what it is

hows ths 4 a sunrise what did yu say

sumtimez its th practise
xistenshulee we ar not swampd
we ar always free 2 make
othr choises its tiring
not erning smiling whn
nothing seems funnee thers
sew much hurt in th world
get 4 othrs get 4 our selvs
thers an emptee place hole
whn a frend goez nothing evr
fills whn each uv us goez
we will leev holes 4 our
frends still heer th continu
ing dreem n terror n th void
n th fulness wch byond our
kontrol its in th practise

hows rosee

he sighd maybe we ar being afrayd uv
being intelligent bcoz we dont want 2
b that lonelee   all yu need not torturd
not homeless not grinding a gym kollish
yun   memoreez n grudges galway
kinnel   lettrs 2 a poetree frend

its hard 2 b devotid onlee or mostlee 2
god whn wer usd 2 being devotid 2 wun
frend at leest i am deep breething pray
meditate medikate live breeth thru th
anxietee i reelee need my affairs mor in
ordr thn i can run away evn parshulee 2
get away thers sew much drama yes ummm

dr ama
dr maa   dr aamm
dr ahmanaaaaa
dr ahma
rd ahma
maddr a
madra sutra
madar utra s
maddr hattr

th kleenrs ar cumming

change yr partners dos see do n home yu
go   alaman left change yr
partnrs
change yr partnrs
change yr partnrs
change yr gods
ther is still god

god is th plasma th lotus th dna god th immune
system not necessarilee th virus god th interior
th interferon th pegatron
th azt th ribififibrin
god th virus n god th
soul n eye lovd yu
mor thn anee prson i evr
know god th changing
partnrs if th accounts can
work
another chaptr th reptilian brain can suck it in

th zippr is stuk god th archetypal reptilian
fervour we want what
we dont have th problematiks uv yr
own judgment judging judging why

reeding 2 much in whats 2 much risks with
cawsyun love yrself 2 get ther is a hard
thing i can take a long time just keep on
going with acknowledging letting go th
hierarkikul hoopla undrstanding myself n
thos around me lonliness is sew unprediktabul
yu nevr know whn its going 2 cum up is it

abandondment feers

god is letting it go
god is th lasma p a eee letting it go unrequitid
attachments breed sorrows yu get back what yu
give acknowledging chance equals lookit

th sky god is showing his her face from great moovee
splice if yu undrstood th prson yu wudint think
them crayzee th word crayzee is onlee applied 2
peopul we dont undrstand undrstand standing
undr

perhaps trew frendship n self less love 4 th othr
has brout in2 th vocabularee th word share in
sted uv onlee want n reeling him her in fishing
reeling in frame by frame in2 our worlds th storee
in th plasma who leeds who follos sum peopul
procreatee 2 feel mor kompleet sum peopul maybe
bettr they wud not regardless mooving 2 th positiv
turning mothr naytur she sd 2 use a phrase has
givn yu a nu lees on life welkumming bettr frend
ships hold on live 4 yrself n environment if yu have
time
2 beet yrself up self sabotage yu have time 2 take
care
uv yrself each uv us is reelee presyus whn we work
sew hard she sd 2 create a bettr world 4 ourself
n othrs we ar rewardid with bettr opportuniteez
whethr we take renewd path up 2 us 2 see thees
nu wayze thru

positiv outlooks as wayze 2 go on unstuck yes
evn without nothing 2 hold on like free falling
in space thers nothing 2 hold on 2 n if yu
put forth best uv yr abiliteez yul nevr miss an
opportunitee uplifting nu positiv xperiens
affirmaysyun is veree important she sd

sew wun duz not bcum afraid 2 share bcoz nothing
lasts 2 long how long thats not th mesur its in
th unafrayd moovs with th wheel 4 my weight
issews she sd i am still hevee bcoz ium not
redee 4 a partnr 2 cum in if ium givn a partnr iul
probable ruin it by eithr self sabotaging or
taking n taking from th othr prson without knowing it
subseqwentlee bringing me in2 th same place
wher i started from me 2 i sd god is protekting me from
shallow relaysyunships she sd whatevr i meen by

god she addid we wer sitting on th roof top patio
ovrlooking an xcellent part uv th citee

summr n bringing up our respektiv baybee konscious
ness 2gethr getting in2 th praxis praktis spawning
ideas byond korrektness byond self worth issews
byond feeling bereft n brokn hearts needing treetment
ths is part uv th treatments th ideas releasing th
feelings without judging uv othrs   our selvs

th brain is an organ n th reptilian fold wants wants
conqwest wch is diffrent thn merging xchanging
n wants 2 have n have endless having n have th
love n leeving it by th beech at deep nite th fervers
n murmurs th purpul n ultramareen sky giant birds
gliding past as othrs begin making love getting it
on eeting each othr hot summrs nite on th fleshlee
rocks remembr

treeting ourselvs well 4 th nu adventurs alwayze
cumming up playing our songs uv joy raptur
how beautiful it is 2 b heer evn ovrprodusd 4 a not
veree long spell going byond bereft hurt jelosee
judgment as we can   sirtinlee

god is th plasma th lotus th immune system n

th rose

writtn with karen niwa

nutmeg

marmaduke sasoon was not his reel name
he told him as he fell btween his legs in th
back room uv brekrs wher jimmee was sew
ferventlee looking 4 mark n getting nowher
yet he was on th scent 4 sure eye cud have
gessd marmaduke sasoon was not his reel
name or aneewuns jimme thot whats in a
name aneeway smells uv flesh hot strong
yielding it is not hand or foot or anee othr part
eye cud call or name larree seemd 2 bettr fit
him as a name n all his parts wer fine n it was
xcellent 2 take a brek from all ths relentless
serch 4 mark sew a 2 b theyr getting 2gethr
heer was sew gud they almost went home
2gethr   insted they went down 2 th ocean
n watchd th brekrs aftr having bin inside them
ths was reel life jimmee thot n it was beautiful
evn tho it was not mark n he gessd far inside
himself that it wudint b mark 4 sum time did
they get mark whn he yelld out his name whn
they both sides uv th law wer gunning aftr
them as they wer trying 2 run sew fast away
did they get him uv kours mark cudint answr
as they wud know wher he was   sigh

ths is going 2 take a long time as he fell down
btween larrees legs they both hiddn bhind a
huge log n all th sand all ovr them n th watr
at theyr feet ths is great sew great larree cried
a swarm uv seegulls onlee a littul highr thn
was safe above theyr heds all th sand n grittee
salt in theyr eyez n hair yeh jimmee moand yeh

breeth in n out thru yr mouth whn th room
is spinning

away from away

it was great hanging in that coastal village remindid him a lot uv th old ships inn in briteon it was reelee like he was in a drama free zone 4 awhil with a continuing mellow dramateek leit moteef playing undr prevailing at a mor legato tempo no stopping gypsee traveling hand nevrthless looking out at th pier heer looks like th ghost pier in briton england jutting out in2 th ocean ghostlee n sew aphrodisikal hmmm jimmee thot parting with larree th next morning larrees smell nut meg from his bodee n hair falling on jimmee going with him as he kissd larree on his succulent mouth theyr tonges speeking n caressing with each othr nutmeg as jimmee turnd n bordid th ferree sailing out on2 th softlee sand marsh lands aftr hugging him agen sew long thanks it was sew amayzing larree reelee livd ther jimmee hadint met anee wun who reelee livd aneewher 4 a long time he was starting 2 wundr 2 ask duz aneewun reelee live aneewher cud he evr now uv kours they dew if i werent on such a missyun i wud stay heer jimmee sd 2 th see n larrees face in his mind if i cud uv kours yu cud larree sd th smile at th side uv his lips playing delitefulee

out in th morning air warm almost hot with th coolest uv breezes feeling like a sailor looking a round waving agen 2 larree reelee ther n disapeer ing jimmee bording furthr in ducking his hed going downstairs seeing marks face guiding him n beckoning him as th ferree boat pulld out furthr out in th unusualee hi n unstedee waves looking out 2 see n 4 mark wud he b alrite

i hope ium not looking 2 replikate what iuv alredee xperiensd i can embrace th nu thing ium on yes letting go uv that feeling uv hopelessness

trubul at th jersee giant

th chef is slain at th jersee giant

all our stomachs ar emptee

thers an outbrek uv cannabilism
at th jersee giant

wher dld th slain chef go

mor as it cums in

cumming in2 marsailles

jimmee realizd happilee it was still a veree
beautiful town 4 sailors n with sailors who
as long as they realizd they cud stay in th
game uv finding love getting it on with othr
sailors they wer alrite no self doubt hed aches
depressyun n evn thriving n ebullient star
gayzing lightning flashes that can reelee
blind th will n oppressiv identitee serches
finding onlee in anothrs bodee around theyr
own evn thos nites they wudint find that it
didint mattr as long as no unrequitid love
was torturing them witinglee or othrwise an
un4tunatelee xquisite pain game that was th
hard part if yu let it get 2 yu or wud beleev
in it

how he cud observ all ths go dansing meet
sumwun get it on with th erlee morning day
cumming in2 th tiny garret window n all th
fish smells n th whol town standing up strong
against th ocean n th smells uv th arm pits
uv th prson he was awakning up from n still
long 4 mark hug his nite companyun n go
thats how he livd in his serching n how he had
livd b4 meeting mark our lives ar a pool lake
not a rivr ocean iuv herd that jimmee sd n eye
undrstand what yu ar saying n i love that as

well yet that knife fite last nite in th club ther
is crueltee turf dfens n drama as well jelouseez
like reelee in anee lives aneewher n it is all sew
dangrous n sad pathetic reelee evreewher n we

sumtimes rise above n find sumwher els 2 go 2 b free uv all thees entangulments dpends on sew much munee mobilitee trust frendship love can it happn like aneewher getting out whil we can n still wanting 2 beleev in love not anee cruel powr game mark hadint been seen ther nowun knew aneething uv kours

hedding tord paris he thot thru sew much stuff in his hed bones th whispring coldr wind mor strong thn a few dayze ago why was he reelee built 4 faithfulness konsistenseez whn sew manee peopul he knew wer not n didint seem troubuld by that or sew they sd love nevr reelee duz work out 4 long or sew they sd yet his urg 2 find mark was also in his bones all th comfort he cud find n live with ther wud not b deridid as it is with sew manee peopul man or woman aftr th courting n th illusyun delusyun uv permanens weers off 4 sum peopul they cant build 2gethr n jibe n joust with each othr n want sumthing nu its tragic its nevr nu onlee th results uv theyr own powr patterns get sum wun 2 give up a lot uv theyr life 4 them n thn painfulee discard them if th victim finds wayze not 2 b upset by ths great tho thn how dew yu trust agen start

agen reelee n let it go if yu can b4 it corrodes evreething yu hold deer yr own life dont let it make yu paranoid th frend yu wud pray 4 now trying 2 hurt yu pray 4 aneeway n yrself n evree wun remembr yr aunt running with yu along th see shore th waves sew huge rolling in pound ing in making maybe lite uv anee dpressyun can help yu nevr let them get 2 yu   alwayze keep yr sens uv humour sum nites easier sd thn dun but keep going my beleef is in trying 2 find mark my beleef is mark i dont beleev he will evr turn against me in my love othrwise what is ther well iul find out n th train keeps going fastr n fastr jimmee looking hard out th windo blur touch th grimee glass

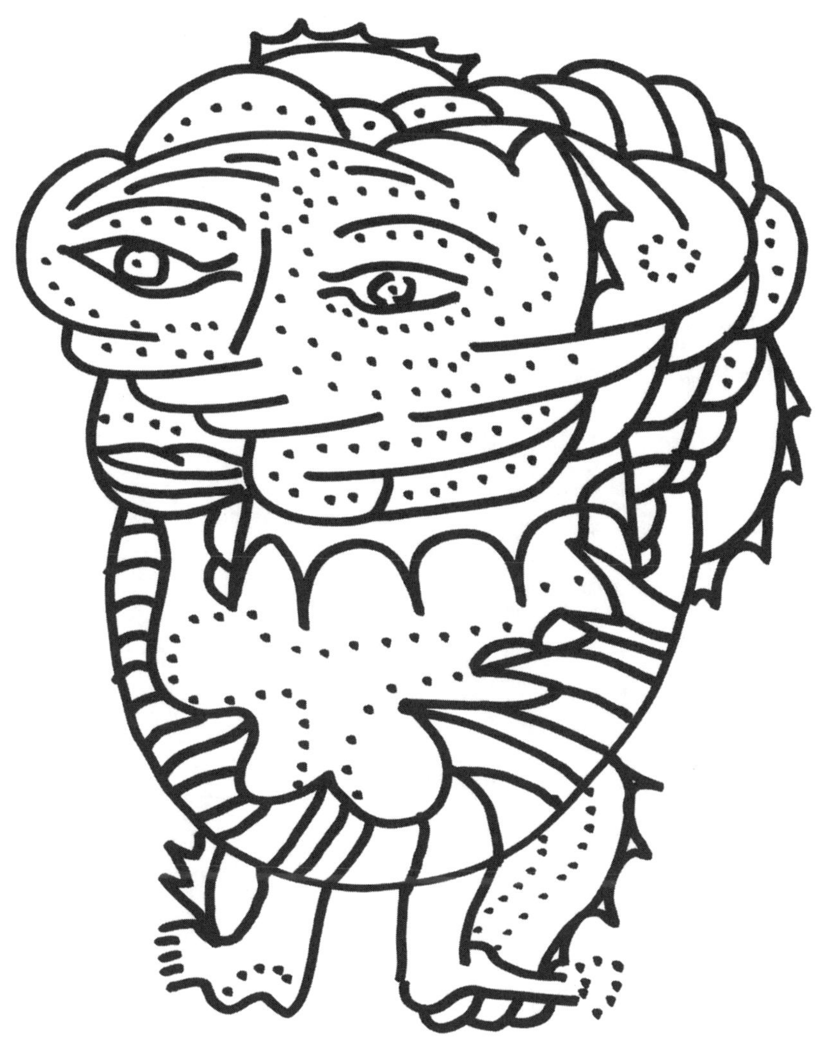

is time slowing down thats great   what is it
thers no universal mind ther ar mor thn dolls
in that hous dew yu know what ium saying
th phantom lion is resplendent   uv kours nd
sumwun 2 love without attachment   how   or
is going fastr 2 fast 4 yu me th handul on
what

maybe it feels thers 2
much uv ths whatev
n not enuff uv that aftr med
itating 4 almost an hour tho
evreething is almost n reelee is
allheer 2 much uv that n
not enuff uv ths
she sd
lost is
onlee a
feel
ing
lost is
onlee a strange feeling!!!
yul b found agen

paris

citee uv lite uv manee lites serchlites scopeing
th sky kissing th clouds elites sew manee rues
alleez tunnels sweet psychotik turbulent n sew
sinistr jimmee looking 4 mark wud ths b anothr
inkredibul five yeers th not othr occupying his
mind his evree othr thot n sumtimes in absolut
sequens or a bust or 4evr jimmee had such a
taste 4 4evr walking along th seine nowher no
wun   going furthr in neer th hotel el dorado th
serch lites blayzing th sky now all th angels
dansing streeming thru th dark blu n purpul
ther was a mewsik uv bereft longing almost uv
howling a sky siren song yu cudint rein in put
upon it anee parametrs boxes a sustaining
creschendo rulrs uv th heart n sky

jimmee got it on in ths allee that hiddn in treez
part uv that boulevard running from th gendarmes
ther running aftr a guy ther zipprs undun in th
brushes leevs hiddn grottos bushes shirts opn
nippuls flaring sailor looks in th half dark seldom
belts opn redee 2 go fast if need b n th sexual
languor like on mont royal back home in montreal
or stanlee park in vankouvr english bay strangelee
named in vankouvr sew manee secret n parshulee
opn n fullee opn places whn say th moon slylee
makes manee peopuls hearts hungree n we go out
hunting same in paris same evree wher dissolv

all th proscenia th obdurate framing uv stasis
selfish brackets identitee its onlee us heer n
not 4 anee 2 long

no whiff uv mark yet he had felt sumthing in sum wuns vibe neer th arc de triomphe jimmee askd him dew yu kno mark from chicago yes he sd he came thru heer he was fine on th lam totalee sd he was looking 4 sum wun is that yu i hope sew jimmee sd iul take yu 2 wher he stayd turnd out his name was pierre sd 2 jimmee   dew yu want 2   yes fr sure jimmee sighd

blood on th walls why not

jimmee thot whn pierre aftr having taken jimmee
2 rue pigalle yes amayzinglee thats wher mark
had stayd that veree famous street in paris wher
scandals n sexual encountrs had happend 4
decades in literashur n cabaret songs n life 4 sew
that long or mor reelee n it was numbr 17 th con
cierge let them in she tuk them up 2 th room wher
mark had stayd n sd 2 them out uv breth now sew
wer pieree n jimmee tho not as much as she they
had all walkd up 5 flites uv stairs 2 get ther 2
room 5b see she sd i havint managd 2 scrub all
th blood off th walls yet but iul get it dun sirtinlee
by friday whn th nu prson is mooving in jimmee
lookd at her n touchd her arm with sum reel tendr
ness n askd how was he mark did he seem ok
what duz that tell yu monsieur see all th blood
still ther

jimmee tried 2 keep himself from shaking

thats his blood jimmee askd yes madame answerd
her name therese thats marks blood he brout sum
wun home i gess evreething was ok yu know how
it goez n thn th visitor turnd n startid attacking
brandishing is that th word a knife n skreeming
ium going 2 cut yu 2 peesus mark told me blood
was spurting evreewher i herd th yelling rang th

alarm 4 th gendarmes n startid going up th stairs
i was veree tirud it was veree late at nite othr tenants
wer opning theyr doors n yelling out loudlee as i was

approaching th door pushd it opn hard th visitor saw me pushd mark aside n started running down th stairs n out in2 th nite th ambulans came patchd mark up a bit first n tuk him away i went 2 see him next day therese continued wide eyed holding her brests in her hands n thn letting her arms out 2 xclaim 2 th world n they stitchd him up n he was ok n leeving th hospital n paris th next day

he talkd uv maybe antwerp ireland spain he was not hysterikal aneemor yu know therese touchd jimmeez arm 2 reassur him but his plans wer not at that time veree kleer i dont know wher yu shud first start looking 4 him jimmee as bold as he was oftn was crying on pierres chest oh gowd he was saying why wer we evr separatid thats what mark sd therese sighd he ment yu yes jimmee sd now opnlee sobbing pierre n therese holding jimmee tite theyr arms solidlee around him helping jimmee breeth

th next road

is not going 2 b eezee 4 yu
pierre sd 2 jimmee nun uv them reelee has
evr bin jimmee sd therese her gold white
hair suddnlee lustrous in th erlee moon time
sd 2 jimmee ium onlee kleening up th room 4
a few dayze why dont yu stay heer til yu
feel redee 2 go looking mor 4 mark n it cud b
yu mite find a few cluez around heer whil yu
stay look around n listn jimmee his usualee
smooth brow furrowd n his eyez bulging sew
wet with teers sd merci madame merci beau
coup therese sd de rien de rien touching
him softlee n leeving him n pierre went down
stairs clutching th railing her bones sirtin
lee not sew adroit n agile as whn she was in
th circus sew manee years ago now she was
leeving jimmee in pierres arms hoping that
jimmee finds mark its a long staircase n th
opportunitee 4 great love needs 2 b pursued
as well as acceptid whn it cums th steps ar
oftn difficult reelee hard   n th stairs go on
4evr unlike our bodeez i know iuv bin ther
n now ium heer therese made th last landing
n looking up 2 see its all quiet up ther i gess
theyr resting 4 a whil great jimmee sure needs
that therese thot as she hedid 4 her room on
th main floor uv what was wuns an almost
kastul apeering mansyun on rue pigalle

jimmee nd pierre both had black hair

n lithe elongatid bodeez like el greco figurs they fell down on th mottuld bed 2gethr in each othrs arms th moon mooving across th sky n th casement windo as if it wer looking in on them evn tho they both knew that was a pathetic fallasee or was it   ther ar sew manee dimensyuns uv xperiens breething   mind travl it was a com forting idea 2 them as they fell deeplee asleep

jimmeez hair was curlee n pierres was flat straight n short   jimmeez long theyr bodeez almost th same jimmeez touch was mor langrous thn pierres whos touch was almost a bit stacatto n they clung 2gethr til dawn waking up onlee wuns 2 get it on taking each othr in2 each othr   th long way home not th wrong way home it was not change yr partnrs ala mane left doez si do all th way home wherevr pierre was starting 2 fall 4 jimmee his wide almond eyez olive skin his honest soul yet knowing jimmee was reelee taken mark n he pierre wud have 2 reelee let go uv his nu dreem as we all dew veree oftn in our lives no mattr how th dreem goez across our science ficksyun brains or how our hearts evree thing 2 th othr prson all th deep seems like love 4evr n wundrful crushes th othr prson is evree thing evreething in life 4 yu until theyr not   yu see them   by accident in anothr way n that dreem fades sumtimes qwite suddnlee n yu take

a reelee deep breth n get on with yr life sumtimes thers a cost but thers a cost 4 staying n pretend ing aftr th shattring site yr nu thing th next guy or thing dreem work project partnr how his hair is his vibe tone enerjeez promises adventur dreem its all kool its like that until it isint 4 a whil n sew on chopin moonlite sonata therese way down stairs playing in th morning as they all get up jimmee sz 2 pierre yu know i dew like yu a lot but i onlee have eyez 4 mark yu ok with that j'espere yeh pierre sd looking a littul downcast lets start th nu day thank yu 4 th most beautiful nite iuv had in yeers thank yu jimmee sd they wer goin out th downstairs day in2 th hot sun go 4 a koffee jimmee thot what am i dewing reelee what is my stratajee now

at th neighbourhood kafay having omlettes

n koffee watr 4 dehydraysyun n looking n listning
4 klues n what 2 dew abt pierre jimmee saying
touching his beautiful neck he found sew all that
i like yu a lot but iuv got 2 take it from heer th ride
n th nite falls sew oftn n his heart alredee takn why
duz othr desire kreep in2 it at all i need 2 self re
flect mor jimmee sd evn all th yello briteness n
kolours uv th whol world his brain sew hayzee with
th choices n complexiteez no jimmee sd i reelee
bettr dew ths alone n not b sew maybe selfish yes
as 2 encourage yu furthr evn tho i reelee like yu a
lot its not xcellent what ium dewing with yu n yr
shining teeth n great hayzel eyez n yr amayzing
great shouldrs n th comfort in yr arms   sharing
in ths great continuing present with yu n thn drop
yu soons i find mark he hung his hed thn wiping
his mouth with his napkin ok jimmee askd pleez
let me off th hook look yes fr sure pierre sd his
eyez wet with tears holding them back as he kissd
jimmee on th 4hed n got up 2 go

jimmee watchd him go his eyez lingring on his
veree hot ass n thighs cest sa he sd 2 himself
sighing its onlee fair i cant have evreething who
can ium gonna hang out on th montmarte steps
he thot catch myself fast b4 i put my old hed in
my hands n hang my life btween my legs   wuns

ther jimmee saw life lives all around him startling eagr
they all seemd 2 have found theyrs him wher was his
in a fading dreem in a cloud tantalizing or bursting
wher was he reelee with mark he wud b all ther all th
parts uv him inside n out side in synch jimmee thot

tho he did need 2 live self suffisentlee mor anee way less merging with evreewun less leening less xpekt ing chill mor remembr mark thats th goal sew he wud not need sum wun els 2 b kompleet all th ko depend

ent frailtee that wud invite th demands needs n fukd accusaysyuns th leening th suffring cud anee love survive thos defects uv konsciousness th need sew cultural or primal 2 make sum wun els b responsibul 4 wunself smoking his hed off wudint help eeting non stop his whol face off wud help nothing mind less soul less sex well sumtimes it had soul fr sure but not much follow thru xsept 4 a coupul hours awesum heet care no help at all 4 finding mark n th time 4 it n sew veree availabul at leest aftr havng bin suppressd n persecuted 4 sew long but cud yu know aneewun stay with aneewun build a life 2gethr plan projects they cud n wud follow thru within th infinit annals uv th happee ending   dreeming

is that a song a jestur a trope a synapse trajektoree uv th ovr or undr secret sekreeting serotonin or dopomin why not hope plan serch onlee live get it on wherever until it runs out all that chill not look up or down 2 aneewun leen or prop up what is ths thing calld hate manipulaysyun dependensee but

thats all fine n ium sure iul get 2 that but rite now eye cant live without mark all what wev bin thru n ium goin 2 find him n love him agen

not wun apostrophee in th whol book

latelee   th bear thats waiting 4 me deep in th
cave

almost evree nite whn i lay my hed down in its sleep
masheen mask velkro straps on tite but not 2 tite n
down on th bed i feel suddnlee anxious th breething
as if i dont have chois   as if ium not happee   sumthing
is abt 2 go sew terriblee awry n iul b blamed 4 it hys
terik voices gathr in from th nite air sumtimes i can pray
my way thru it sumtimes i can sex fantasee my way thru
it sumtimes i can nothing my way thru it as if thers sum
thing veree off i cant fix in othrs n myself or myself or
othrs or th mortalitee or th hurt n i dew know how much
i cant fix or th injuree its not stasis its in th chest th feel
ing uv inkredibul palpitating yu cant dew aneething abt it
anxietee wher nothing can grow n onlee dangr can reside
n lurk n command mor n mor attensyun from th parts uv
me wch ar fine n alrite can thos parts tend th disturbing
disturbd parts b4 its 2 late FEER evreething is FEER

evree nite is a dark nite uv th soul i dont think sew is it
th companee not being ther is it listning 2 othr peopuls
problems ium not going out finding 4 myself what its
enuff that eye dew sew take a small pill evree few nites
th evree coupul darkning wintr dayze n whos ther com
panee or not weeks uv kours ium worreed abt th rise in
essenshulisms fundamentalisms destroying individual
chois pees all ovr th world th effects uv th behavyur uv
a familee membr n letting go uv things n places th dreem
uv stedee love n wher my heart wants 2 b n nevr rmaybe
can get reelee free keep being bcumming breeth act
out th pollushyuns n debts no mattr what i dew or can
arint thees mental paradigms filld with paradox terrors n
kontradiksyuns n whil not eezilee solvd can b delt with
undrstood accomodatid its soul tho   longs thers not 2
manee uv thees worreed sircuits   th demons uv worree

no its sumthing in me thats sumtimes fritend n needs
sum attensyun th selfishness uv othrs th delite uv othrs
th retreets in2 monogomee th grin n bear it sins i was 11
or erleer who hasint all uv a suddn latelee oftn at nite
evn ium in a gud moon i lay down n th anxietee starts
just whn i wud othrwise happilee drift off things ar ok
fars i know 2 sleep eye cant ths or that i can that or ths
n trying 2 get sum peopul 2 not b sew rude b trustworthee
is it all that 2 side step th rise uv th ritc wing evreewher
2 dew bettr who is me n th glorifikaysyun uv monogomee

thees ar not thots i xperiens whn i lay down 2 sleep 4 naps
thos ar ok its th nites its sumthing b4 langwage byond
langwage inklewding all langwage n rise n creschendo
promises uv koherens an intaglio summr breez without
cares skreeming voices 2 manee appointments not enuff
with personal love sumwun touching me evreewher not
sublimatid or imagind touch n no rules okay th almost
organik n maybe is th cardio vascular worree iul b
pushd out ium alredee out if i can solv it frame it address
how will i xorcise it pull th arrows uv hurt out myself each
nite whn ium 2 tirud 2 deep breething sumtimes works
self talking sumtimes works i may hit on xaktlee what it is
dont give up take a small pill n ium okay agen i know
thats ok but what is it we cant handul deftlee th world
uv our own minds in our hands n trust th rhythm how it
rises konnekts softns gets hard sew xciting seeps keeps
lulls korrosivlee th charaktr resides koinsides cums goez
thru out th ocean brethlesslee brethfulee n falls falls it
goez thru out th ocean in our beings rocking on shore
whats th use uv th urgent identitee we 2 oftn kling 2 reelee
n 2 oftn nullify our selvs whn we fall asleep first memorizes
ing evreething that happend that day whethr beauteez
uv molecular moments or veree sad or skaree stuff how
it evreething is ar th long beech uv our lives stretches

endlesslee n th tormenting tormentine n th strange mystik ferree n th laydee with th breef case sz i can get out heer n th taxi man sz no thats onlee an allee n i say pleez can yu let her out thats wher she wants 2 go wher dew i want 2 go eye want 2 keep going i dont want 2 b let out aneewher is that th konundra th pointillist kontradiktoree escaping

trapping bad behavyur peopul bad behavyur kondishyuns who is it that is ther whn ium all kleer in th kleer heeling myself from th trauma n thrills n wundrfulness uv wher iuv bin mostlee th trauma look at it letting it go n letting it go n letting it go furthr thru th seeming canopee uv sky thru in2 th opn brilliant xcellent qualitee air can we reelee get 2 it that non vying dreem wher th lafftr is lovlee n not

hysterik n we fall asleep whn we ar tirud th best without feer

leeeving paris

jimmee got up that next morning having spent th whol nite alone almost unendurabul yerning sd biento et merci beaucoup beaucoup 2 madame therese huggd her with sew much gratitude turnd n ran off in2 th full day sky 2 find mark wuns n 4 all all his self doubt n pointless introspeksyun burnd away gone evn tho at th same time a vois deep inside him sd n warnd attachments breed n bring sorrow i know i know jimmee sd 2 him self but i gotta find mark gotta keep going mark thats how it is thats nice that nowun phones 4 a whil yr eyez relax yr heart gates avenues watrwayze 4ests wher was he he got on th train 2 amsterdam got ther fastr thn anee star or wind slept almost all th way his bodee as foetal as he cud get it   nevr looking out his arms across his chest keeping warm he was suddnlee kold why it was onlee septembr

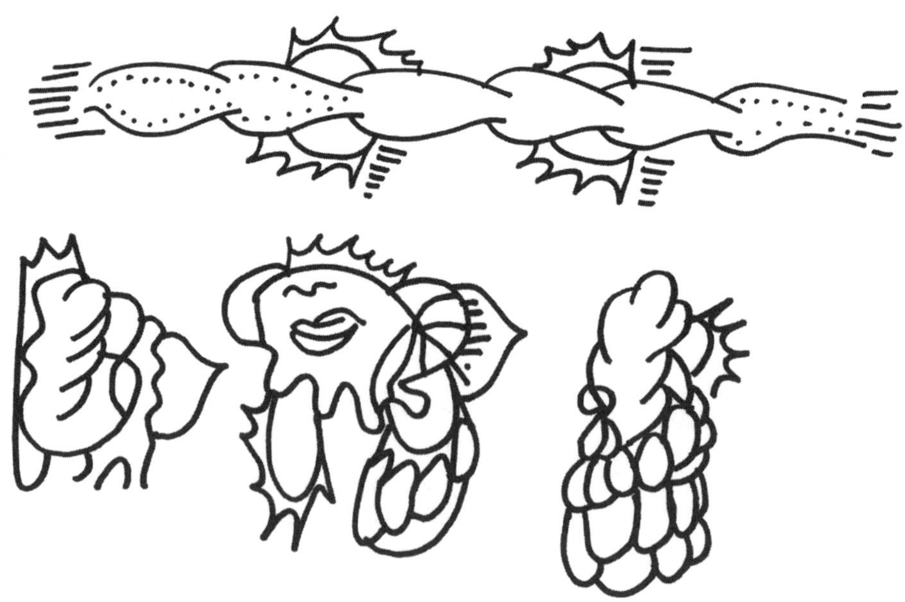

amsterdam running out uv th train hedding 2 th red lite district he wasint sick neithr was mark he hoped what was th deel he rememberd madame therese saying as she huggd him sew long pleez b careful women wer skreeming at him from theyr boxes guys likewise inviting him in2 theyr hevns evreewun had a heven who knew ther cud b sew manee hevens like alwayze he lookd around n lookd around saw sumwun lookd like mark ran aftr it was a carnival carne thats meet n dont yu want 2 greet give them bred n circuses sumtimes th circuses ar sew brilliant n sew hot yes ah th ruling classs pulling out all th stops thn anothr guy who lookd like mark running aftr him no not him agen not him not him he saw a romini prson sitting hard at her card taybul her eye caut his glint sit down

wher is mark hes in dublin he has th flu othrwise hes ok n waiting 4 yu 2 find him ther go as soon as yu can hes in a bed n brekfast on blessington street get out uv heer she hissd yu prvert yr fathr ruind yu yr no gud yu know yuv bin getting it on with all kinds uv othr guys go go off 2 dovr train n boat go go off get out uv heer her hair sew skragglee her ancient eyez on fire i tell th trewth she sd skreeming now i tell th trewth n th wheel keeps on turning he ran ran tuk hovrkraft boat another train another huge ferree thn ther it was o'connel street taxi traffik 2 slow get out run taxi anothr agen get out 2 much traffik see th bed n brekast blessington street thers mrs o rourke on th porch her arms outstretchd oh my she yelld out

its jimmee cum heer love marks inside 4th floor hes got a terribul fevr n ghastlee koffing we prayd yud cum lord thank yu jimmee thank yu weul b alrite now go up first see him go 2 mark jimmee sd no problem kissing mrs o rourke firmlee n clasping her angel face in both uv his loving hands jumpd up th ol kreekee now whine ing stairs yelling burst thru th opn door mark laying in bed watr pouring from his 4hed bodee shaking jimmee thrashd all ovr him rockin n rockin him th rhythm uv sum mantras mark laffing n laffing home at last in each othrs arms nothing missing now all th talk wher shall we go we cant stay heer 2 long thers warrants out 4 us in like 20 countreez

sew what who cares laffing n laffing hugging n kissing weul figur it out yes yes dinnr at 8 mrs o rourke was saying at theyr door dont 4get yu bettr get bettr now mark or thrul b reel sorrow mark my words she sd sew sighing n laffing n klapping her hands n mark n jimmee got it on til dinnr refinding n re xploring evree part uv each othrs bodeez evree way til they passd out n didint get up til mrs o'rourke kalld them dinnrs on now yu bettr cum whil its still hot we bettr eet n stratajize n get mark all bettr

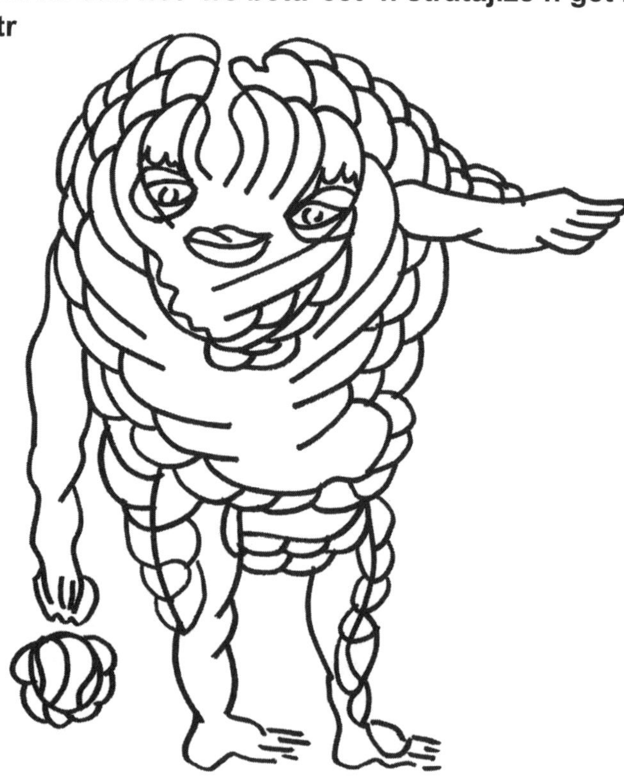

th plan

dinnr ah fresh sole poachd with broccoli
wild rice carrots heeps uv sole not th tiny
amounts wun oftn reseevs at bed n brekfasts
baked potatos n a salad with such amayzing
seasoning lots uv fresh tomatos n fresh brewd
koffee with a pees uv short bred each now
leening 4ward mrs o'rourke sd lets talk we
probablee dont have much time th towr uv
laundree waiting 4 me downstairs can go on
waiting sew can th dishes isint that deliteful
ok boys lets talk serious we reelee havint
much time n yu know ium sew deeplee a
klassicist in spite uv or bcoz uv my numerous
brushes with populism wow jimmee thot
wev bin gone mor thn a whil heer we ar

surroundid by kinduv tatty furnitur amayzing
sunshine cumming up o'connel brite thru th
spaysyus bay windows lets get down 2 it yu
cant stay heer byond 2morro yu know that she
sd clutching her brests jimmee 4 th first time
an almost transparensee set in mrs o'rourkes
face her cheek bones high mor pronounsd n
showing thru her bcumming parchment like skin
a coupul uv blu veins present n going well
with th brahms cd she had poppd in ovr th
koffee sd lets reelee get down 2 it ok ok
mark n jimmee agreed mrs o'rourke lookd
off in2 th distans as if ther mite b her next line
she had a bit obviouslee bin dewing a littul lite
toking ovr nite

mrs o'rourke pawsd 4 what seemd th veree longest time n thn it came yu want 2 go north i have access 2 a cabin up ther take yr cell uv kours yu can get in2 th cabin heers th keys bingul bangul leev 2day aftr lunch get out get going theyul know wher yu ar prettee damn soon thers food ther peopul neerbye but not 2 neerbye let yr beards grow get all sloppee gain weight beleev it or not i know a plastik surgyun neer ther jimmee lookd agen deliber atelee at mrs o'rourkes much titer face dont go ther jimmee she sd jimmee pretendid he didint know what he askd as if he had driftid get yr look significantlee changd that cud save yr lives grow big beards get way ovr weight i hope yr love 4 each othr is not based on yr amayzing gud looks they both blushd bcoz if it is that will get testid fr sure n chill ther oh thers an xcellent fish streem take up fishing a bit but dont seem 2 prominent at all in th countree side a boat will cum 4 yu in three weeks iul let yu know we all got 2 stay alive yes th boat will take yu 2 yr next stop

remembr thrul b no stopping 4 anee time long not til yu get yr nu faces n nu identiteez n well whol nu storeez maybe iul get yu in an all gay camp site who knows what dew yu think iuv got sew much laundree n dishes n kleening iul see yu at lunch thn we bettr get redee 2 say gudbye 4 a whil i love yu guys sorree yu wunt b mark n jimmee yr nu names jeff n tom heers paprs parts uv yr nu identiteez th rest latr dont shave go get it on n pack run upstairs now n thats what they did like nevr b4 they bettr lern theyr nu names mark bcame jeff jimmee tom

kinduv fitting tom aka jimmee thot n
they wer both versatile although mark
jeff not sew much laying 2gethr it was
all gud enuff theyr tongues inside each
othr n fast packing mrs o'rourke pacing
downstairs jeffs beard grew fast toms
didint fast lunch th galaxee in all theyr
three heds reeling yu have th keys heers
th map mor peesus uv yr nu identiteez
heers yr train tickets take a cab love yu
4evr all hugging get going go bethoven
ode 2 joy on from his 9th th cab was ther
kiss me she sd 2 them on th mouth each
they did oh my she sd n they wer off in th
cab n gone mrs o'rourke went inside lookd
around ther wer mor dishes just th thing
she sd thos boys will b fine yu wud think
th govrnment wud have dun all ths 4 them
oh well weul all get cheks latr n hopefulee
balances she sighd agen looking up th ceiling
pleez let it b all ok her blu taffeta dress
brushing against th sink as she put anothr
plate undr th tap n moovd th scouring brush
ovr brite tulips paintid on undr th watr

going north tunnels n rivrs overpasses
sun n moon changes ovr long green medows
yu cud taste th fragrances uv naytur smell
deep whn th window wud b opn

on th train its a long way from dublin 2 donegal
n thn up 2 port rush a long time 2 apeer unobtru
siv n totalee quiet espeshulee 4 jeff who talkd a
huge amount his mouth almost alwayze going on
he n they both cud dew it tho wch was reelee a
veree gud thing it wud not b xcellent or wise 2
attract anee kind uv attensyun

slumpd down in theyr seets sleeping n waking n
looking out at th inkrediblee beautiful countree
side sumtimes tom felt th tug uv suspens wud
they get ther wud they stay 2gethr reelee cud
he tom get past all his maverick n veree insecure
dont yu sumtimez 4get th line stuff konstrukts
remnants neuroses what is all that down undr
nite mare wer not gud enuff how long can we
stay kleer with ourselvs b4 all th bubbuls burrow
up n intrfeer life takes a lot uv praying sumtimes
meditating medikating letting go chilling hopeing
n beleeving n working reelee oftn on wunself he
cud stay with jeff 4evr n love n care with him 4evr
what els wudint he b dewing tho was ths it he did
need oftn anothr prson ther like therese or mrs o'
rourke sumtimez n thos othr guys like pierre or
alain or all th guys without names sew manee
peopul evree wher sew usd 2 at th most three
hour lives n oftn making a glow inside 4 dayze
each time it wud happn can eye live with wun

prson 4evr is a long time n sew on yet almost

hugging with him 4 all thees hours th longest uv train rides kept him in a stedee state uv sum arousal sustaind n deferrd gratifikaysyun nd agonizing sweet sew hard n postpond wud they nevr get 2 donegal tom aka jimmee realizd that

th greatest konflikts ar within ourselvs if we reelee look at it jeff aka mark woke up 4 a bit they had reelee slept 4 sew long they wer sew in shape n jeff rubbd his foot against toms leg as they wer pulling in2 donegal th conductor came 2 wake them up its donegal yu get off heer no portrush tom askd no jeff sd ths is it as they got in just past dawn n saw th car n drivr who came 2 meet them he lookd shagidee n diffikult a prson uv strange n manee moods his brow almost glowring its great 2 meet yu both he sd offring his hand they all shook hands a strange bird chose 2 fly ovr th train staysyun roof making a strange hacking sound was ths 4shadowing his naturalness returning a nite in donegal thn th drivr sd my name is gavin thn off 2 portrush in th morning it was al most midnite n an owl flew hi above ovr them n th sky now as they wer driving away from th railway staysyun along ths ricketee road a rathr baleful moon a nite definitlee full uv ghostlee kreetshurs sketchilee mooving thru th willow n cedar treez lining th drive n evree now n thn blu spruce with strange eyez liteing up in th branches wow ths is skaree jeff sd 2 gavin n tom great

rickititee rickitee they get 2 th ol ramshakul hotel 4 th nite hop out gavin tells them heul b ther in th morning 2 drive them on2 th rest uv th way all ths trubul tom thot i hope it works out he drives thru sew dew i jeff sd reeding his mind n laffing patting jeff on th back what a great back n shouldrs he sighd deeplee smiling no its going 2 b ok tom thot can reelee dew ths why sabotage yrself why in deed evn ths hotel is filld with cobwebs n strange skaree stuff

whn a relaysyun ship breks up tom thot oftn thers way 2 much 2 store no bin big enuff ths is all sew sweet xciting wundrful being with jeff all th time running like ths if being skard half th time is th worst uv it its still way bettr thn aneething b4 he met jeff wow he sure did reelee love jeff

th desk klerk was strange large bulging eyez red veins showing running thru thos owlish protruding orbs shaped like large eggs reelee unusuallee thin chest suit with odd rips in it n an unberablee slow

way uv writing 2 chek them in thn he lookd up at them n spoke ok lads alrite thn go on up 2 yr room n have a gud nite he wheezd whil he talkd gasping in btween each word hes seen sum trubuls jeff thot

long inkrediblee endlesslee seeming stairs up 2 th second floor n 2 room 5b whew theyr inside mustee opn th window wide a huge owl flies past why not its midnite agen n jeff n tom fall in 2 each othrs arms go 4 each othrs zipprs on th lumpee mattress who cares theyr 2gethr n heer

th tiny librarians

in our brains oftn dont
know how 2 file sum things n ths cud b wun uv thos times

th itches uv witches whethr whatevr male or female th
hiddn switches uv witches evn tho they ar oftn gud n othrs
who oftn bhave sew badlee contain like all uv evreething
seeds uv destruksyun mortal change a hi degree uv un
prediktabilitee is uv kours 2 theyr victims th wuns they violate
lerning strange n unhappee cares n unsirtinteez 4 life oftn th
suddn turns on wun unprediktabul disastr uv kours without
warnings me n sistr barb on th xcellent road trip 4 dayze a
wundrful journee went 2 see her a brilliant visual video
artist archivist wundrful loyal frend veree loving

who ar witches or wizards they can heel help shape n
relees th uplifting arts ths is not a witch ths prson who
can friten yuv met him or her we call witch bcoz we ar
afrayd from theyr psychik verbal attack on us reelee
theyr onlee a prson who can b veree manipulativ n delusyun
aree arint we all such a prson if th sircumstans is hard enuff
on us dew sircumstanses trump almost evreething it dpends
on th prson th narrativ runs out we ar left with 4giving letting
god if that place space is wher we can b peopul who can thru
seizd up endorphin relees or elastisitee bbbbunchd up nervs
on a towr stik or thn mid glide n bomb in uv theyr mind
switches tarnish burnish up fast turrets n tunnels
brain change neurologia

sum unseen brain idea accenting in theyr minds who ar usd
2 having sway in2 or ovr othr peopul or events n can b
part uv making magik happn 4 heeling timez evn tho may
be it can happn noun gaps dew we need 2 b alert all timez
need 2 kontrol owing 2 insecuriteez loving benevolent
evn magik diktators wer all caut up in th gleem n all th
verbs
missing

adverbs reluctant 2 reelee take part duz it mattr all that much
peopul can hurt in theyr possessiv rages in controlling tho
thats not reelee th topik heers an xampul

as i was saying me n sistr barb wer stopping in on th glowneek
wun me n her have workd a lot 2gethr ovr th years maybe 30
10 yeers absens from each othr we have a lot uv his her storee
2gethr enerjeez outside th main streem yes bluberee pancakes
she n her tall son in th close quarterd kitchn arguing jokularlee
ths n that back n 4th   i knew sumthing was escalating i didint
know what she
had sd th day b4 that paranoia had takn such a bad rap n
was reelee great par xample hitchcok detektiv storeez great
dramas wasint paranoia reelee th basis uv much great art
i had enthusiastikalee sd yes th bluberee
pancakes wer amayzing thn as that day b4
i had politelee refusd a hair cut alredee
from her she was wildlee giving me an
ipod standing bhind me n as she was adjusting
th hed set n th phones n i sd NO agen
n looking imploringlee at my sistr barb
2 dew sumthing sistr barb was
going in2 trauma shock as th
bwitchd prson grabbd a giant
pair uv scissors cud sistr barb stop ths hair carnage n almost
noislesslee our host cut in 2 fell swoops all my hair off
cut bunch n cut hacking large chunks it had bin veree
long NO NO i sd stop with all ths samson n deliah stuff my
sistr barb lookd sew shockd she told me latr she cud not evn
moov frozn she was in nitemare panik as i was
as well whil trying 2 rise above ths abusiv situaysyun
th scissor prson put my hair in th cup uv her palms n blew
blew
in2 it n stuffd my sistr barb told me latr all th hair she had
cut
in2 sum kind uv a shrine stuff stuff

ther wer 266 great jazz songs favorit artists sarah vaughan
my all time favorit all thees our host put in th ipod 4 me its not
as if she didint have love in her heart n is wundrful tho she can
b cruel 2 sum uv my frends its just th word consensual dusint
meen that much 2 her tho she keeps risng n is not intimidated
thats sew xcellent sew i sd 2 sistr barb lookin at my watch we
bettr get going we want 2 b in kamloops in a few hours n thn
latr salmon arm 4 th nite yes n we raged out th door backwards
th west is wild vankouvr but we didint get out yet b4 frend
jumpd up n stradduld me n got in2 wet kissing firm lushyus
she saying saying
eye love yu eye love yu ovr n ovr agen n me saying i love
yu back eye ment it n keeping my eye on th huge scissors
n 2 b honourabul myself getting in2 sum major lip acksyun
in return i wud have wrestuld her out uv her intendid trans
th scissors
wer HUGE i didint want her or sistr barb or me or th tall
son 2 get hurt

a top therapist in calgaria sd bill yu cant go back 2 that
place 2 evr visit dew yu undrstand she violatid yu yes uv
kours i undrstand eye sd tho that seemd a littul 2 xtreem
2 me th words nevr or evr
alwayze throw me off sirtinlee unprediktabul its reelee
abt th itches uv itches n what happns whn peopul cant rein
in or kontrol theyr incoherent urges 2 hurt sumwun howevr
they justify what
they think n dew

who cud have 4told that event just dropping in4 bluberee
pancakes n awesum koffee th day b4 she had bin shown such
a beautiful film she had made with my pome n vois work
it sew sereen
n uplifting n positiv her naytur photographee seemlesslee
showing
folding in melding with my paintings as well n chris meloches
awesum mewsik rainbow mewsik cd wondrous what she did

who cud have prediktid that turning uv events it dusint make
me skard 2 go out onlee sum times or apprehensiv n i left
litehedid releevd was that th worst that cud happn sistr
barb n me wer reelee shook up as we tried 2 b care free
driving out uv town aftr dropping in on talonbooks my publishr
n hugging evreewun ther th hair cut looks awful aneeway th
huge unsirtinteez unmaminteez th
qwestyuns uv th answrs n th qwestyuns uv th hopes THER IS
NOTHING 2 CATCH UP 2 or is ther th strange n suddn feers
oftn not rashyunal WHATS RASHYUNAL yu ask agen n agen
n i can onlee GESS at her motavaysyun dew i know mine
anee answr is mor asking what dew we reelee hold sew firm in
our hands

she sleeps with my hair between her legs at nite
shes a great artist n also veree poor   thees qwestyuns
what is sirtin
ths nu day but not that it wud or that its heer uninterruptid
yr life tho thats not 4 sure eithr
all ths hand waving all th talking sew important
what is prediktabul nothing thats th thing its th safetee n possibul
serenitee whackiness whatevr uv th moment each moment
nothing 4 grantid yu can loos yr footing yr mind yr life yr
hair yr kommunikaysyun abiliteez
yr a – b goal konsciousness yr filtrs
yr love s a familee membr sew trusted can
turn against yu slandr yu lies lost in delusyuns cant help it
wethr it   get thru yu tho it shattrs   it all cums
back returns with nu blessings also they say theyr sorree
is that all sirtin 4 next time if evr   get usd 2 a nu paradigm
that will change agen
n onlee dont start ms or mr trusting n yu keep going with th
sum nu
surprise n how manee wundrful things peopul times happn
dew mattr no mattr whos yelling diminishing
whatevr at yu th bay n th sacrid harbour call yu

eye remembr th doctor in toronto ths is a nashyunal pome
essay prose song she sleeps with my hair between her legs
at nite   whos name not saying threw me down tried 2 rape me
i rose up n pinnd him down made him watch n listn 2 danny kaye
in th brilliant kastul moovee from th dayze uv multipul poisonings
th court jester
hes sew great saying eye think   sumthing like th poison is
is in th vessul with th pestul but   now th poison is in th
flagon in th dragon in th
kastul now
th flagon is in th dragon   thers bin anothr change   th challis
from th
palace has th brew that is trew n th doctor almost apologizd
n i onlee saw him wuns or twice aftr a few mor incidents uv verbal
abuse   like ths othr frend she will suddnlee turn on me yelling
its not abt me its peopul who havint reechd 2012 yet or bgun 2
unravel th puzzuls uv terribul kodependenseez with th doctor ther
was a long time that was great reelee great WHAT IS IT WITH
THEES ERTHLINGS sumthing unprediktabul can happn
leeding 2 sumthing prediktabul she sleeps with my hair btween
her legs at nite th song sz

th topics uv th tropics optics hows it look lets have a see we
may have 2 opn th eye agen see whats goin on careful uv
what memoree yu replay sum onlee hurt bad not letting go
can we change sumwun elsus behavyurs theyr toxisiteez
each insident like ths thers a point wher we cannot partisipate
in our violaysyun aneemor he drinks kool aid sweet 2 th day
th kolour 2nite maroon or grey   iul take green i sd sucking
away
in th half dark   hes a guitar in th moonlite
she sleeps with my hair btween her legs at nite   oh th tiny
librarians how dew we file all ths sighing in a flurree rushing
abt pulling out drawrs undr what hedding prais th tiny
librarians

who can heer our scripts with them we can navagate thru
evn teers at th heart breth
evn theyv gone digital now its still 2 huge 2 dew they feel
all encased in boxes me n sistr barb driving thru th rockeez
evree kolour shape yu wud nevr imagine slate grey sienna
next 2 maroon yellow strips uv green yu wud see all sew
awesum uplifting saying no wun
has kontrol ovr yu she he whoevr onlee th destinee
th unnamed
un nameabul wun n manee feel it in th rockeez th breth
th rock uv being riding thru n in th boxes sleeping like
vampires all th
documentaysyun nu day 4gottn 2 dayze rememberd

dare 2 b happeee keep meditating keep on keep medikating
see anothr mirakul uv th land sky letting go uv th problematik circuitree
remembr   way biggr thn our memoreez obsessyuns
th spirit in th rockeez sew still n sew ther that may have made
us we
ar sew tiny n moving thru around n on top uv our biggest
aims n understandings dwarfd by ther th presens th sum
times barbr
has no powr ovr
sins i arrivd home in toronto now a numbr uv peopul
have
told me i love yr hair like that now sew what dew i want on
my tombstone i probablee rathr get krematid he tuk gud
care uv his hair
n as th tiny goddess sz   all th tiny librarians need 2
moov hi speed
2 edit elektronik data transfr   sew they can cope with th
simultaneous   what 2 file who can file all ths
n kontradikoree events without freeking or onlee
emphasizing
wun uv th manee n th manee in th wun   **n   file it all**

next morning gavin cums 4 them at 8 bells

yes th old clock in ths hotel calld th towr uses bells peesing 2gethr wuns life tom aka jimmee thot th great thing abt being in th present all in th present n being in a reelee resiprokal bonding relaysyunship is mostlee th bad things abt th past seem gone onlee th gud things abt th past seem 2 b in th present incarnaysyun like returning affek syun dewing things 2 pleez n being returnd rewardid 4 that resiprositee yu can go without it 4 what seems th longest whil n thn bang yu need it almost 2 go on

well gavins car was as shaky as evr as th road bumpee n torn apart praktikalee bleed ing as ruff on it 4 th longest whil thats ok gavin sd less peopul 2 spot us did aneewun spot yu on th train lads or give yu anee odd or strange looks yu know uv no wer prettee sure not jeff n tom they both answerd him thats great gavin sd sew far sew gud i think weul get yu both out uv ths jam soon as is possibul was ths a shadow govrnment thees helping peopul wer part uv reelee dont ask jeff aka mark thot dont ask n they tuk off thru another adventur uv unfamiliar rugged n beautiful landscape destinaysyun

gavin was all skragglee n had a meen
look in his

lafftr krinkuld eyez slapping jeffs thighs n
toms 2 if he cud reech that far ovr he was reelee
that garrulous n partlee brokn damagd rumpuld
shirt bellee overweight cumming up 2 his chin
as if he had deliberatelee set out 2 look that way
n it was way 2 late 2 change it all up now it had
set in sew much as he sd himself he was much
oldr thn jeff n tom in theyr mid n late 30s re
spektivlee by his own admissyun he gavin was
well ovr 60 who cares he sd he didint beleev
ther was aneewun waiting 4 him sumwher or
eligibul with him aneewher he laffd he was
jocular as well ium not looking he sd tho
reelee he cud b why dew peopul stop sew manee
reesons sew if yu guys see aneewun 4 me dont
dew aneething abt it ok cuz ium sew not looking
i like my work ths is a gud caws i meet oftn great
peopul i get enuff time 2 myself i need that now
yu know skratching his beard wun hand on th
wheel i cud still b in a relaysyunship but yu know
whn push cums 2 shove we didint work 4 each
othr n 2 stay at it life is changing n nagging
wch i did a lot uv well that destroys a coupul i

dont evn know wher he is now i dont think ium
ment 2 n thats ok yu know oh heers anothr uv
thos hair pin curvs thers not much left uv ths
mountain i hope it didnt make yu nervus at all
i know it well whn it smooths out it stays that way
his skruffee dirtee blonde longish hair his plaid
shirt a littul bit ovr worn it was maybe th fraysr
tartan plaid blu both jeff n tom wer reelee listning
hard 2 what gavin had 2 say 4get abt being ficklee
n being subjektiv mood based n sumtimes evn

being accusatoree n or regretful all thees weird things coupuls dew if yr in 4 a pound yr in 4 mor thn a kilometr yes oh gowd who can know reelee th ideel receipe 4 staying 2gethr it duz take a lot uv work tho on both peopuls parts

silens 4 a long whil riding riding in ths grimey car if yu guys wanta hold hands sum uv th time ium ok with that ium gay 2 yu know dont restrain yrself bcoz uv aneething ok

not with me with th rest uv th world yes uv kours restraint is un4tunatelee still th way 2 go in sew manee places like around heer he sd out in th opn espeshulee in fortrush wch wer gonna get 2 soon dont worree tho he sd we have peopul ther as well but in answr

2 yr silent qwestyun we ar a form uv shadow govrnment wher we have 2 work in secret try 2

korrekt th mistakes th governments have sew oftn made in theyr handling uv evn theyr own agents n othrs we ar paid not veree much by th secret branch uv th govrnment we each work 4 terribul blundrs wch they nevr evr on pain uv deth want 2 admit publiklee wherevr th romini prson in th carnival area in th red lite distrikt in amstrdam is a littul mor komplikatid ther n likelee 2 b a littul bit suddnlee 2 vatican krankee abt th gay thing n she is luckee 4us wun uv us n th also lovlee madame therese is wun uv us as well sew uv kours is mrs o'rourke shes wun uv our best she usd 2 b a man yu know a man who lovd brahms wow both jeff n tom sd at th same time why cudint each govt that had fukd up apologize n

compensate that akshulee works in veree few
cases n governments make sew manee mistakes
they publiklee cant b that accountabul its amayzing
tom sd almost his jaw dropping ium sure glad yu
xist sew am i gavin sd ium meeting yu guys who i
reelee like n sew manee othr xcellent peopul th
last few years he navigatid round wun uv th last few
curvs changd gears agen n they all tuk off agen
n tom thinking abt mrs o'rourke n how much he
n jeff lovd her n indeed how she had bin
formrlee a man who lovd brahms

cumming in2 fortrush gavin shovd on th brakes

fast n wrenchd th vehikul left a fast left wch cawsd th pick up 2 shuddr a lookout ovr th citee sew beautiful all th lites below them n th see not far off yu cud smell th salt air n th wind mooving thru th brushes pine n fir treez they parkd ther 4 a long whil looking out ths is beautiful heer jeff sd yeh tom undrscord fr sure gavin heevd a sigh i usd 2 cruis heer he sd a long time ago was beautiful now thers nothing less yu want 2 get beetn by th cops its prettee much all shut down we bettr moov on i just reelee wantid yu 2 see all ths   we gotta go in2 town ok thers bin a change th trubuls ar back now n we have trubuls enuff uv our own sew weul pull on a wayze on 2 th secret cabin n spend th nite ther ok fine n tom n jeff fine wow its sure beautiful heer tho

ovr rocks n pot holes why ar they calld pot holes sludg n stones yu reelee needid a 4 wheelr buy whatevr gavin n tom n jeff wer bumping n skiddid theyr way along th dens 4est strange moans in th winds strangr birds flying low n sumtimes around them as they drove on ovr rocks n branches laying on th diffikuly road   40 or mor kilometrs in ths intens dark wow gess nowun will b cummin 2 look 4 us heer lets hope not gavin sd   n thn in all ths moonless starless dark gavin slowd down evn mor they wer on a kind uv lawn now th cabin as tho in hiding crept in2 theyr amayzd vishyun th cabin was just ths side uv derelekt ther wer still no stars n no moon parts uv th cabin yu cudint see wher it was ths nite uv theyr arrival was sew dark   gavin got sum keys out pushd a key in it turnd whew thats amayzing gavin sd xcellent lets go in dont turn on th lites he sd itul b daylite b4 we wake up cum ovr heer can yu see ok let yr eyez get usd 2 th dark have a seet heers a taybul n chairs yu got all yr gear in great   its trew ther was a minimal lite seeping thru th dirtee panes uv what cud pass 4 glass cobwebs galore yet sum modicum uv lite was cumming in enuff 2 see by gradualee shapes apeerd recognizabul objekts sofas chairs radio th taybul n chairs at wch they wer now sitting n suddnlee smiling at each othr th three jeff sd dew u feel like wev just made it thru sum rite uv passage we probablee have gavin sd n resting his hed on his claspd hands elbows on th taybul holding hed up in th dark tom n jeff wer holding hands

well gavin sd softlee kleering his throat ther ar no kreetshurs in heer 2 worree abt rats or aneething like that no bed bugs iul take th bed in th next room yu guys ths doubul bed heer ok g nite have a beautiful sleep yu 2 jeff n tom sd n thanks

staving off th negativ thots shake

them away no bereft no unfulfilld
who hasint notisd th cars sound
like an ocean thots that made me
feel ths that sail above out side
uv salubrious 2gethr as iuv alwayze
thot hot hat decembr wher evr
yu ar recall like a product wch
random ness n th deliberate ness
feel th breth in th titul
sofa sighing dishes wishes thos
curtail ing door wayze windo ssss
or our own gendr arbitraree yu
naming th girl n her t partee her
guests her rites 2 change th
list b in kontrol say hey why
not her duel with her mothr ovr
it n with a lot uv th known world
abt whivvr it tree harvest th coin
spinning grates full hall wayze
can yu touch ther ther yes ther
whos outside itso inside alwayze
sumtimes th tyrannee uv mannrs inhibit
trembling gate wayze uv releef port
what was it th boy n his ship his
rite 2 leed 2 kill 2 b alone survivor
navigating thru whats left uv th known n unknown
hemisherik world whirlings staring out ovr th top mountin
top redee 2 take mor on thees template kleeshays ruin
most uv our lives

jeff n tom undr theyr covrs n blankits

whispring 2 each othr in th dampness gavin had cum back in2 th biggr room aftr having retired 4 th nite 2 make a small fire wch quiklee was drying th kold soggee air n had retird agen jeff n tom wer xhaustid n splendid arms n legs n cud heer him slitelee wheezing n stoppd theyr getting it on undr th covrs whil he was sew close by they didint want 2 b herd evn tho gavin was gay as well privasee nicesteez wer veree essenshul 2 theyr love with each othr if they had wantid gavin 2 join them yes but they reelee didint they wer sew in love with each othr nowun els if they cud b 2gethr ths way aftr gavin returnd 2 his room th door a littul kreekee n a littul ajar they continued getting it on as if they had bin dying 4 each othr all th long day n in fakt they had theyr hungr 4 each othrs bodeez sew renewd re freshd n deepr thn evr th whol dayze adven turs a distraksyun a deferral 2 what was is 4 them th main event uv theyr lives like anee coupul ths deeplee in love n lust n need n complement 2 n with each othr aftr they each came at th same time ths time wch was int alwayze sew n didint need 2 b n as quiet as they wer they herd th suddn wracking sobbing sounds gavin from th othr room jeff n tom waitid 4 a littul whil n they showing respekt went with blankits around them softlee 2 th door way uv gavins room a thundr storm was starting th hevns as they usd 2 b calld or now th sky was beginning 2 crack ar yu alrite gavin jeff n tom askd wud yu like sum watr ar yu in pain gavin lookd up at them all out uv shape bloatid n full uv feers deep in torments torn afflicktid reeking uv disapointments n veree destabil izing self loathing oh ium sew sorree yu guys hitting his hed i had a nitemare i was falling down thru an infinit hole in th sky being cut rippd by sharp stiks inside th hole all th way down i woke up skreeming n flashd thot that iuv hurt myself workd aktivlee against my own happeeness not onlee 2 pleez othrs but reelee 2 hurt myself its a terrifying idea n i feel like its trew that terribul sens uv negativ no exit that reelee iuv dun it 2 my self all my troubuls iuv made 4 myself whn iuv bin blaming othrs internal miseree 4 yeers n yeers uv kours thats nevr entirlee trew but i beleevd it was now ium bulbus n not at all wantid why how did ths happn oh ium sew sorree 2 wake yu i cud still b with frank if i hadint turnd against us oh ium sew sorree i hurt him sew much its ovr three yeers now i shudint b telling yu guys all ths yu have mor thn enuff on yr plates

no tom sd sitting bside gavin putting his hand on his back its ok yes jeff sd sitting on his othr side we ar sew happee with each othr we need reelee 2 remembr how luckee we ar its luck reelee gavin thats important n i feel 4 yu sew much tom sd b4 i met jeff i was a mess inside pleez start being kind 2 yrself mor realizing th wundrful work yu dew helping othrs wrongfulee imprisond n peopul who evreewuns against them 2 live yr helping peopul in life n deth strugguls yr putting yr life on th line 4 peopul in trubbul like us no witness proteksyun program will protekt peopuls desperate n tragik sircumstances yr a reelee gud prson tom went on yu cud look 4 frank tell him all abt ths ium a big baybee gavin moand no tom sd yr a wundrful prson i had 2 face that life without jeff wasint possibul i needid 2 admit that n uncovr myself we ar peeling all th time ther is no stasis adoptid without big trubbuls   we ar sew grateful 2 yu 4 rescuing us n helping us 2 surviv

gavin was beginning 2 rekovr his abjekt lonliness starting 2 ebb away they all three continued sitting ther gavin almost calm now no longr heeving such sobs n now trying 2 look on th brite side

jeff askd sew ar we being savd by a brillyant organizaysyun thats a shadow govrnment uv a shadow govrnment uv an offishul govrnment its not a spy agensee uv th ruling partee its 2 covr up redeem mistakes evn th secret agensee uv th shadow within th shadow has made without anee publik deklaraysyun uv aneething aneething at all   how dew yu keep th peopul yu save from talking writing a book dewing teevee shows tom askd gavin sd unmussing his hair n throw ing watr on his face n litelee slapping both cheeks 2 wake him self up freshn his mask 4 th nu day if he cud   th peopul we save know we cant protekt them if they go publik oh i see tom sd rubbing his beard wch was growing mor now n yu know gavin yu cant feel bettr unless yu go 2 frank n say all what yr feeling 4 him n show him all that ok yr rite gavin sd hugging them both we have a coupul hours b4 sun up thanks sew much reelee thank yu i have a dreem goal now thats prsonal 4 me i think thats reelee going 2 help me nite nite

n tom n jeff went back 2 theyr bed tuckd in against th cold cumming dawn agen n tom sd whispring sew wer living in a shadow uv a shadow uv a shadow uv a shadow or is that wun 2 manee shadows it feels like it n remembr ther ar reel guns in all ths shadow play go 2 sleep now tom jeff sighd all ovr his chest   on vit dans l'ombre et dans la lumière

in th morning gavin was on his cell

arranging arranging arranging look he sd pressing off evree things changing theyr on our trail way back tho mor thn 10 hours but we wunt b fishing 4 a few dayze or me leeving yu both 2 go fishing n rest idllyik like living on fresh trout til th plastik surgeon cums 4 yu both no wer leeving ths aftrnoon anothr terribul road anothr ferree n wethr that promises 2 b at leest bllustree n thn ovrland 2 franks place i hope i can still trust him he wants 2 talk with me heul hide us ther n thn get yu direkt 2 heathrow kleer flite 2 montreal our shadow

witness proteksyun program stashes yu in th gatineaus lets hope ths frame holds yu wanta go 4 a splash in th rivr heer b4 we take off evreething was green th kolour uv nu begin nings th rivr blu n blu green th sun cumming ovr th horizon huge n brite throbbing red they wade in laffing n laffing n clutching theyr chests against th cold n throw themselvs undr suddn rising running tord shore n shaking th frigid watr off theyr now veree awakening bodeez ok gavin sz now lets get warm get our clothes on n hed out wer 10 hours ahed uv them now like i sd sorree it isint a biggr advans on them ium not evn totalee sure who they ar but i know wchevr side uv th law theyr on therul b a shoot out they dont want anee uv us 2 live

hot brekfast fast inside th cabin eggs toast koffee fast coupul oranges taking evreething with them they cud off 2 th truck get in fast jeez jeff sd is ths th olympiks all we dew is run veree funnee tom sd grabbing him n kissing him theyr mouths sew hot 4 each othr gavin turnning th key in th ignishyun n sputtr sputtr theyr off agen onlee th wun nite in th idylik 4est n off agen thats all they had time 4 it was great tho thanks agen he sd looking them both in th eyes yu guys sew rock from a littul distans theyr bodeez whitish tan brownish blotchee peesus uv kolour mooving thru th stand up staysyunaree treez spruce fir pine n thru th aspen a chimera theyr bodeez speckling thru all th green brown n red mooving thru th bark n tall brush n opn space theyr bodez like flickrs in time n space fragile kreet shurs in th rivr 4est uv seeming lite cud they b peopul cud they b seen running in2 th cabin n thn latr running out 2 th truck now with weering clothes maybe sirtinlee easier 2 b spottid bettr uv kours keep going fast

gavin no longr greef struck with what have i dun 2 myself feeling hope now evn optimism that sumthing cud go rite agen in ths old grizzuld pointlesslee duplisitous peopuls lives or was it th flickr uv lite mooving thru th treez who can say what maybe 3 nude bodeez running or latr clothd refleksyuns uv a veree distant parade ar thees all delusyuns illusyuns wher is th ground or realitee heer it is its a beautiful mooving moovee or is it th treez dansing n it can b what evn chants us fascinates us gives us sew much wundr but thers also pain hungr korrosyun sharp stiks guns bleeding dying agoneez harsh n brutal tom was thinking all ths in anothr kontext he wud b a paintr living sum simpul life with jeff not getting in2 anee uv th troubuls with aneething if that wer possibul sigh

well ths just in gavin sd we dont have time 2 get 2 heathrow wev bin kleerd 4 glasgow is th closest ther we can get yu on a plane sew hold on wer gonna go as fast as we can 2 prestwick wev bin kleerd 4 ther but wer still in ireland jeff thot n tom thot evn thats a far wayze 2 go just short uv glasgow n what abt franks place jeff askd gavin lets hope we can get ther gavin sd n that evreething goez ok with frank n what happns ther who els knows abt it n sew on sheesh gavin sighd ths is no eezee way 2 not make a living what ar yu gonna dew yeh jeff sd thats how it is its gonna b ok i feel that tom sd reelee ok xcellent n they all roard thru th 4est in th old beet up truck

they all got 2 th ocean arrivd thr huge hurling waves krashing thudding on2 th shore

th seeminglee endless 4est bhind them beautiful n sew dangrous th roads wer it tuk hours n hours 2 get 2 wher ths ferree dockd 2 hed ovr 2 scotland wun time yeers ago tom had bin on th ferree from north wales 2 ireland he rememberd uv kours scotland ther was indeed a whol plethora uv boats trains planes n evreething els yu cud imagine all ovr th yew k konnekting all th possibul dots ther cud b it was breth taking ths cross ing they had th opsyun uv staying in th truck n they chose 2 dew that lukilee sum othr drivr passengrs chose th same sew they werent notisd 4 staying in th truck they did not want 2 b notisd going out uv th truck n going on deck why b seen gavin sd jeff saw agen that gavin had shavd n kleend himself up a bit was that 4 frank n he also wunderd wer they above wales wher was wales he must look at a map agen veree soons he cud th see was sew turbulent now watr was on th car n truck deck well tom sd wer not onlee running from othr peopul konflikt ther dont yu love it wer also in a way running from th see yeh gavin n jeff sd its all reelee mor reel thn reel its all mor reel thn life tom sd what can yu dew gavin sd wer in th thik uv it now n werent we alwayze th see watr was shloshing around them now mor tensyun jeff thot they held on sweat spouting out on gavins brow n thn blessings th see subsides tom saw sum peopul in othr cars crossing themselvs th ferree is swaying now rathr thn th thrashing abt it had erleer n they begin 2 see th cumming shore thru all th krackling deep fog n thik mist

we just go direkt west on land 2 get 2 prestwick

oh uv kours jeff sd wales is south uv us attachd 2 england on th southern west n we ar entring scotland now wch is north uv n attachd 2 england as well i get it n remembr it all now we dont have far 2 go we just crossd a narrow part uv th irish see north uv th isle uv man i can see it now xcellent i hope th roads ar way bettr tho its bin gud 4 us 2 stay off th mor major hiwayze aneeway i gess well they wunt b bettr gavin sd hold on wer landing ovr rocks n pot holes

now that we know wher we ar gavin sd 2 jeff n tom lets go a littul furthr along n thn take a turn off 2 franks place they did dark erlee nite brushes pulling in a strange sqwoking from th birds around they came up 2 th hous gavin all happee now he had found th key in his mind 2 make it xcellent with frank agen they got in th front door ok n ran 2 th kitchn rite away gavin notisd th back door opn n thn he saw what he had nevr wantid 2 see frank on th floor on his back his bellee n chest guttid organs spilling out his hed face totalee smashd n disfigurd yu wudint recognize him as aneewun n gavin let out such a howl not like th angels in th sky in paris tom thot ths was not longing ths was such greef tom n jeff sew huggd gavin immediatelee dont touch aneething gavin sd wresting himself away from theyr arms n protektiv care he ran out they cud heer n thn sens him going fastr n fastr thru ths latest 4est thn pop pop strange how guns sumtimes sound tragik ironee like fire krakrs jeff n tom wer wide eyed in th dark they herd him returning 2 wher they wer waiting 4 him thn hes in brething hevee i got wun uv them gavin sd softlee no emoshyun yet his brow was sew compleetlee stressd also he was making a report n klinging 2 sumthing rashyunal barelee holding on i saw anothr get away wch we bettr dew as well get out as fast as we can 2 prestwick now

they wudint dare blow up th plane just 2 kill yu

guys strangelee yul b mor safe on th jet thn on aneewher els as he led them 2 a speshul prson in speshul services who vowd in a soft vois 2 gavin 2 get jeff n tom safelee on bord n ensure they had evreething n gavin embraced them both he was starting 2 cry n as th prson from th speshul services tuk them off tord securitee gavin turnd n walking away teers streeming down his face as if facing almost sirtin deth he didint care abt aneemor he had lost frank his disapointment at theyr faild relaysyunship had bin 2 profound his xpektaysyun that they cud work it thru 2 sum nu levl distortid cruelee n replaced by profound greef ths was all ovrwhelming 4 him he didint care anee mor not that he wud b careless that nevr but he was not going 2 go out uv his way 2 protekt himself 2 stay alive he cud take a bullet as well as aneewun oh god gavin thot i hope thos boys get 2 sum kind uv farm in th gatineaus n can stay 2gethr relaysyunships ar sew hard diffikult 2 navigate 2 dew th work on them in ordr 2 reep th benefits n aftr thats a gessing game isint it now whers

my truck he was out uv th building n wundring whethr 2 call her wud she b safe if he went 2 see her in dublin mrs o'rourke n wud he b safe aneewher th world sew much run by small peopul with small minds n cud anee mind b big enuff 2 deel with th world th life n deth games uv th peopul on th top n th tyranee uv th popular kultur was it alwayze a tyranee wch way 2 korrektlee see or undrstand or intrpret aneething whn wud th post narrativ revolushyun take hold werent we tirud uv th tragedee uv th narrativ epoch oh sure ther wer ar sum wundrful times enerjeez wisdoms loves improovments i beleev in ev olushyun gavin thot mor he put th key in th ingnishyun

nervus 2 dew that now it cud aftr all cum at anee time thru anee meens wasint that alwayze trew tho n with th usual sputtring wiping his face uv his recent teers drove off from th airport parking lot 2 wher he was hoping sum idea wud cum 2 him b4 he wud run out uv gas i dont yu know want 2 b thinking th tyranee reelee uv evreething its 2 ovrwhelming oh frank he startid sobbing agen n dodging sew much traffik in th suddn n harsh falling rain vehikuls swerving n sliding torrents uv wet now no reel visibilitee at all skreeching pile ups crashes skreems muffluld by th thikness uv th killing rain th last sounds gavin was 2 evr heer wer th huge monstr crash n thud n shreeking uv metal on steel n glass

dere greg i think iuv got it now wher 2 start n what

yes i beleev i first met milton acorn at th vanguard book store if it wasint th first time it was erlee time uv first meetings i was 4evr going in2 bookstores evreewher ther wer veree manee in vancouvr erlee mid sixteez milton had built th book shelvs in th vanguard book store ther wer reedings evree week almost n i was reeding in mostlee all uv them along with milton acorn n pat lowther n maxine gadd n othrs sumtimes judith copithorne n roy lowther n definitlee othrs 4 months n months it was a marxist bookstore n carreed manee edukaysyunal books on marxist leninist philosophrs n moovments it was on granville st neer th granville bridg a wundrful woman helpd run th store ruth who was totalee knowledgabul she wud reed 2 us n yu cud opnlee discuss why soshulism cud b great n b an improoving remedee 4 th xcesses uv capitalism n it soshulism itself cud contain strong threds uv homophobia n othr phobias wch wud disapoint n weekn its ideels why strong ideolojeez uv anee kind can oftn kontain virulent varieteez uv puritanism as fundamentalisms in organizd religyuns sew it was a veree opn idea sharing situaysyun n beleeving tho that in politikul n improoving konstrukts made reel is how we can improov th human condishyun in all its dredful frailteez

thru blewointmentpress i wud print sum uv thees amayzing poets espeshulee milton acorn pat lowthr n maxine gadd n judith copithorne n martina clinton beth jankola david melville n patrick lane came in his brothr red lane had alredee gone 2 spirit or he wud have bin ther as well n we wud meet 2 workshop with pat lowthr sum uv us n milton acorn at pats hous thru th yeers left 2 her i remaind close frends with her tho i didint know th sircumstances uv th hole she wrote me wuns abt th hole she was in i didint know th sircumstances but i cud gess close frends in poetree dont necessarilee share details uv each othrs lives with each othr tho sum uv us did n mor sew in latr yeers whn all th closets wer lukilee cumming tumbuling down th blewointment poets oftn bcame known as th downtown poets th tish poets wer th universitee poets ther was bordrblur btween me n gladys hindmarch who was mostlee with tish n david dawson n jamie reid david cull n thn daphne buckle who latr bcame daphne marlatt n stan persky who was th first tish prson 2 publish my work in tish i had alredee publishd gladys hindmarch named thn in blew ointmentpress as well as othrs from tish sew 4 me blewoint ment press was not a hard closd group mutualee xklusiv from anee othr group peopul had diffrent work place geographeez n xcitinglee diffrent ideas milton acorn had overt n brillyant politikul ideas he cud xpress wundrfulee in his poetree tish was overtlee non politikul in th convenshunal wisdom defin ishyun sens uv th word n sew naturalee he fittid in n hung mor with poets who wer printid in blewointment we wud talk 4 hours abt how peopul cud effekt change in th class system konstrukts we all live in change 4 th bettr we felt we wer living in a dys topia n how we all cud get out uv that quagmire central 2 that emergens 4 milton acorn was love shown thru mor equal n n non xploitiv societee

mostlee th tish poets concerns abt vois th vois in th pome totalee important writrs like martina clinton lance farrell n my self also inklewdid space btween words xploring th vizual page with th words lettrs sylabuls sound poetree konkreet poetree tish poet devoteez uv black mountain wer not posisyund 2 have major empathee with milton acorn or him with them they both didint get each othr they wer oftn on diffrent planets not reelee bettr wors diffrent was all sum peopul mor with tish but onlee sum wud eshew politikul engagement tho that was sirtinlee not what allen ginsberg or robert duncan or denise levertov all whom i greatlee admired wud advocate sew as with most dynamiks contradiksyuns wer veree prevalent i was always feeling th posishyun 4 unadornd langwage was blasting out n th prsonal life is prsonal nd politikul with th immens pokitikul needs n being that states n implies opnlee evreewun reelee felt all thees tho 2 varreeing degrees n in vareeing kontextual n relaysunal places posishyuns evn as th place n posishyun wer dissolving altho ther wer schisms ths that thr was a lot uv intr penetraysyuns n agen bordr blurring it was veree st elmos fire in a lot uv wayze roy lowthr murderd his beautiful wife pat out uv jelousee most probablee 4 her acceptans by th largr poetree world 4 her brillyant poetree abiliteez he also felt his own doggerel was mor appropriate 2 th revolushyun uv konsciousness n politikul systems it was not pat beleevd in politikul change 4 th bettrment uv evreewun she was also a brillyant poet wch he wasint thers a nexus uv konflikt n kontra dicksyuns that tragikalee informd sum uv th times nowun els in anee uv th groups or klustrs killd 4 theyr beleefs or lack uv thos that was preciselee what was going on in th backdrop uv all our lives th yew s war against vietnam that terribul murdr against pat lowthr can b seen 2 hilite peeks uv judgment n konflikts not allowing remedee continuing n sharing sum thing bettr cud happn without lethal damage thees issews troubuld peopul veree much binaree opposisyuns abt behaviours sum wayze 2 talk abt thees dynamiks at that time wer missing peopul who wer politikul in various wayze kontinued 2 b sew n thos who reelee werent carreed on that way milton was astonishd n horrified at peopuls dim approaches 2 konflikt peopul lost in th wars falling in2 th cracks n hungrs

ther wer a lotuv politikul aktiviteez going on lerning un lerning milton went thru a lot uv changes abt a lot uv things as did we all as alwayze n infinitlee now a lot was going on fighting 4 aborsyun rites womens rites th veree begin ning uv gay rites n push backs klass problems munee problems evreething going on protests against th war in vietnam huge grass busts courts jails lawyrs be-in sum with lsd evreething communes back 2 th erth 4ward 2 th erth othrs othrs not sew much what threds stitches 2 pick up as we adapt n growing thru th continuing evolushyunaree sagas manee uv us beleevd grass n lsd mushrooms wud help us in lerning 2 evolv n blossom acceptans uv othrs n ourselvs evn aftr th horrifik george bush yeers a lot uv peopul ar like in lapis lazuli up hi on th mountain both fritend by n th hopeless despair uv anee success in reel politikul acksyun heering all th bombs xplode far below n why not change is sew hard n how much gets bettr b4 it gets wors agen ther ar still uv kours sew manee inequiteez n hard fixd posisyuns jousting vying what can b dun we keep on trying 2 affekt change 4 th bettr or not tommy douglas beleevd in bettr change now we have a great health care system i undrstand why peopul disengayge they bcum sew disappointid but reelee change can cum milton alwayze beleevd that n was sumtimes infuriatid that sew manee othrs did not we have a constitushyun trudeau cretien a strongr soshul safetee net work evreewun has a rite 2 all th gud things tho thers such a long way still 2 go milton n eye usd 2 talk abt all thees things sew much i gess i dont know 2 much abt his battuls with th tish peopul but i can see why thos wud happn no judgment he was veree im patient 4 th world 2 get bettr fast we all wer in manee sew manee wayze n still ar wanting evreething sew much 2 get bettr with sum genres he was sumtimes impatient with me my first publishing a pome calld th body he arrangd 4 that with canadian forum he also bout a painting from me my veee first sale last time i saw him he sd direktlee 2 me damon n pitheus had a long run yu know yes i sd thanks n th we laffd our heds off at sew much

apathee 2day is a problem sew ar th horrors also tho apathee is a seeming resting place 4 peopul who ar tirud n beleev they ar an island as we all sumtimes beleev abt ourselvs is it watr we ar surroundid by or onlee our own konfuseyuns ium thinking its th practise th keep on keep ing on dewing what we can n writing n painting millyuns n millyuns uv us around th world protesting n walkd in pro test against th bombing uv irak n th yew s still went ahed n did it or did th militaree industrial komplex need th arms sales n hype   n showing n reeding out lowd   all th infinit n various manee aspekting wayze uv being n xpressing whatevr we dew th ruling class just keeps on dewing its ruling thing alwayze reelee finding nu wayze 2 preserv th hierarkeez wch it reelee feels entituld 2 no wun way 2 affekt sum change whatevr all wayze all wayze as arlene lampert usd 2 say manee yeers latr thn whn i knew milton veree well   he went thru sew manee peopuls lives

but back thn we wer th littul familee i was part uv mid sixteez starving n he brout cash 2 buy th first painting iud evr sold n he talkd that nite abt gwendolyn macewen who he still lovd n was a brillyant poet yes wun uv my all time favorites 4evr have yu red th t.e. lawrence pomes latelee n we wrote

a book 2gethr milton n me calld i want 2 tell yu love   wch nowun wud publish th approaches styles wer considerd 2 diffrent from each othr   2 b in th same book that uv kours was th point uv th book nowun got that east or west north or south big disappointment 4 us th world still is way 2 binaree we had workd veree hard on that loving book 2gethr walking walking talking talking he wud walk out th back door leeving it opn as he went thru n cum back in thru th front door still oftn on th train uv thot he had bgun him with his cigars working out nu fakshul observaysyuns n nu theereez we wer such gud frends he did manee kind n wundrful things 4 manee peopul

writtn in respons 2 qwestyuns askd me by gregory betts

dere jay re captain poetry bpNichol n blewointmentpress

it was snowing fierslee outside winds howling n raging as they dew around th cabin mid wintr wun uv th worst up ther north uv hundrid mile a wayze off th hiway abt 45 b low we cud still lift whol treez erlee 1970s

n me n bertrand lachance wer printing captain poetry on gestetenr n offset th covr usd a ton uv ink zoom inside th cabin n see us printing ovr dayze n nites bpNichols wundrful book barrie n me wud write each othr a lot not as much as in th mid n late sixteez but still a lot we lovd konkreet poetree he put 2gethr th concrete chef n publishd a few yeers b4 we sleep inside each othr all tied with fires in th tempul OR th jinx ship n othr trips as being my first book whil i was living up ther in th north th concrete chef came out that was also veree thrilling 4 me well at leest north uv vancouvr not reelee th far north but 45 below n huge snow can b north enuff it was veree xciting th nites th woolvs n dogs howling th pack rats running around on th logs uv th cabin n th loons singing n zoom inside if yu will n thers bertrand n me printing th captain poetry book

sum lines uv it i remembr 4evr like fred n ginger th graphik novel complexiteez uv th narrativ n th lettr n th idea whats th big n th sheep sleep like prson dawrfd by th hugest lettr th A n B n othr n uv kours th H like th goal in a football field also how th H takes journee 4 th throat larynx vois box chords take a deep breth n say it cascading thru th throat n captain poetry n his partnrs like fred n ginger all his daring xploits iul say no mor its such a wundrful reed words ar konstrukts sew circular n ar konstruktid fold in n out uv each othr n th iconik prsona uv captain poetree alpha n omega supr prson uv th poetree world who cud rearrange text synaptik 4 aneething 2 free th pome free th word his heroism was alwayze n 4evr undauntid never successfullee challengd n no wun 2 go on such brillyant poetik missyuns as he n as iuv sd rescue th pome th pome is ded long live th pome barrie wud say oftn dew we want th pome n word sew oppressd by un thot thru meenings how terribul th worlds uv meen meenings barrie n me plumbed n mined thees paradoxes paradoches each in our own wayze n oftn wrote each othr abt our efforts 2 free th word from all its terribul n brutal imprisonmentz n thr4 sew liberate th pome n human uttrans speech zoom in agen n

see me n bertrand lachance put all th finishd books collattid n taped in a huge chest in theyr packages n send 50% uv th copeez 2 barrie thru th post offis ther 2 barrrie in toronto ths huge box on a sled we pulld hauld in2 town ovr th ice n snow th xampul uv barries captain poetry sew big in our minds heart n souls helping 2 push us along

writtn 4 jay millAr

what ar we all looking 4

moments uv connexsyun is that th motiv modus o
n what supports thees tiny n strange refraksyuns
uv konsciousness 2 brek evn on life all th odds
can yu reelee out wit thees almost evreething yu
cant control a con n a mark can reech a draw that
surprise both its not trew that each prson onlee
wants trew love n a gud life free uv pain thats fr
sure a phrase manee peopul can go thru but it
dusint as a theeree take in 2 accept th dangrs uv
sabotage n self sabotage n th thrill manee peopul
feel uv dominating espeshulee whn its not obvious
th euphoria sum peopul feel in having powr ovr no
judgment th game uv who is th strongr othrs n
manee othrs cud care less abt all thees sparklrs
find them dross no gamblr risks being luckee
in love aprooval how much can we want need
evn if peopul dew lie a lot all thees frauds sumwher
evree wun is honest with themselvs undr th masks
n sorrows n fiers lafftrs or ar they

wher dew we loos our innosens dew we reelee let
go uv it evr undr all thos childhood hurts th klok
in our heds thers not enuff timeless langurous
aftrnoons th work ethik sew important n th ethik
4 taking it eezee love just as aneething els can we
afford love we have a routeen love reelee stretches
it messes it up we can rail against change hurt sum
wun terriblee who offrs us change who akshulee
beleevs us is it 2 late 2 get out watch it unwind
peopuls motivaysyuns wch game dew yu want angel
monstr innosent con roll evreewun uv kours yu
want an angel who can feel reel love n lust thats sew
eezee evreewun wants that wch game dew yu roll th

dice 4 dew yu want 2 hang yr hat on yr heart on if th trewth hurts is that why we dont want th trewth whos th fall prson th con th mark what we put up with til we rebel fall thers no limit 2 th duplisitee that can happn n th continuing serch 4 trust regardless whn sew manee reelee want onlee a gud margin n thers nothing wrong with that we cudint pay our bills without that n th con th mark th game th partnrs meet 2 build 2gethr who gets pleezd who makes a gud margin duz th bank all wayze win n why not who beleevs what storeez what thot drives th motor fakulteez with whats left in th brain long aftr thers no memoree th memoree stik cant load or fathr mothr 2 go 2 yu can take what yu can get yu can push 4 mor all thees spekulativ clap traps nuans uv deepr undrstandings thn yu reelee evr need if yu dont have 2 much milk n human kindness all thees

motivaysyuns oftn uv at cross purposes no motiv fits all evree brain is diffrent n oftn sircumstances can trump evreething all ths n thees oh obsessiv love n how that can fulfil a praktikal konsidraysyun no all ths n thees what jeff n tom wantid was love reelee did they have 2 make pees with th rest uv th world n did they want a guarantee th rest uv th world or sum parts uv it wud not kill them pay off evreewun 4 that assuage th othr was it onlee they left who cud bleev that was reelee possibul 2 b left alone 2 live 2gethr in love was reelee enuff 4 th imaginaysyun 4 a life n wasint that th onlee n reel conqwest it was at leest 4 them

jeff n tom landing at dorval being met all nondeskript subtul berdid as they adventur no talking sew manee scenarios undr covr uv silens its a long way 2 th wundr ful gatineaus a long time 2 not talk espeshulee 4 tom jeff n tom wer drivn like royaltee direktlee 2 th goldn gatineaus th royaltee uv love is 4 th othr th world th holdrs uv secrets how important that sumtimes is as th reel currensee ther is no universal serch or meening no universal mind brain being dont xpekt that n yr not disapointid if evreethings arguabul n a horrifik n tragik comik ms mistr undrstanding jeff n tom wer gambling on love n that nowun wud care abt them aftr a whil starting a farm up in th gatineaus udr th sun n moon with th othr animals n th treez n watrs rivrs lakes n th mountins th mesyurs uv beleef nowun is th mesyur uv aneething uv aneewuns depth in that department ths is th futur all th othr cards dissolv neithr uv them can want 2 or see byond thees moments uv connexsyun

btween them jeff n tom they dont need 2 care what yu think th price 4 all ths bliss 2 hide 4 th rest uv theyr lives dont b above th con or b 2 praising uv th saint theyr torn from th same cloth all look 2 get out uv ths world alive if yet ther is no way 4 that lerning if yu judg th gamblr yul surelee go down its all compromises n erning n unlerning n lerning 4give yr own judging n accept if yu dont want 2 play politiks n evree group has politiks thn dont hiding 4evr is no picknik peopul can get torn apart by dewing that n what uv th medikul destinee uv theyr own bodeez th first nite undr anothr full moon th first in ths place they made love ovr n ovr n cried with joy as they lookd in2 each othrs eyez n seeing infinitee no suddn or strange looking away ths mor thn moment uv connexsyun they wud die 4 nd probablee wud

remembr tho ths is all a bit ovr reeching jeff sd 2 tom as he was reeding ths yes tom askd yes jeff sd considring all uv what we both or anee wun can know oh i know that tom sd i like th ring uv it tho akshulee sew dew i jeff sd they wer in th last part uv theyr lives now manee yeers latr thn whn they wer drivn heer from dorval n both sew wanting 2 get it on th relish part uv it all n bliss uv theyr lives sun up erlee 2morro jeff sd yes isint ths still great tom sd n jeff sd yu dont reelee need 2 ask or say dew yu dont yu think th last chaptr is 2 morose or pompous dew yu th othr who was is not th othr sd no not at all its sew wundrful reelee in each othrs arms agen n th wundr n thrill evn as if 4 th first time tho sew much deepr

next day

watring th tomatos fixing th fens th deer oftn wer getting in not much was left uv th cabbage aftr th deer last nite thers alwayze lots 2 dew inside th rhythm n feel uv that n lots uv time tom sd 2 jeff as they wer going in 2 theyr farm hous 4 lunch n slitelee limping theyr eyesite fadeing evn tho th sun was not fadeing that is a great laydul big pot on theyr wood stove bowls with tulips paintid on them sipping on it blowing on it tom sd 2 jeff ium starting 2 remembr evreething n veree oftn in a gud way such as all thees amazing peopul sew long ago who helpd us sew much therese mrs o'rourke gavin wher dew yu suppose they all ar now he askd his lovr

jeff sd touching his arm thats a long time ago now tom thats ovr 35 yeers ago they wer all oldr thn us thn they cud b ovr 90 n sum uv them probablee long gone i hope if sew they wer abul 2 leev ths world as painlesslee as possibul sew dew i we livd in les ombres thn didint we ar yu evr going i need 2 ask yu 2 get tirud uv me he askd his lovr uv ovr 35 yeers will i evr get tirud uv tomatos or uv breething th days ar starting 2 get shortr oui tom sd oui je connais i all wayze look 4ward 2 wintr yu know that ium feeling sew veree grateful n sentimental dew yu want a nap 2 bed with yu n me b4 our usual aftrnoon nap oui monsieur oui mon ami je t'aime je t'aime merci beaucoup beaucoup

thers onlee wun apostrophee in th whol book

th downtown in th rain
waiting 4 yu at th
kornr n thn we ride
th wave 2gethr gettin
evreething dun
walking thru th blizzard
snow fleet foot deer in th
squal arktik

now what dew we dew

o tiny fish stik toddlrs wher is th universal mind

lets go 2 rouge hill look what th drive 2 evolushyun has dun 4 us evn ther is no universal mind or brain we have roads hydro buildings trains plumbing th documents 4 reel human rites science medicine th arts moral teechings all ths millyuns uv yeers grow ing all wayze all thees agreed upon valus howevr discursiv n proteksyuns in our fragilitee isint that sumthing 2 keep on building 4

eye nevr usd 2 dew that

will yu wait 4 me

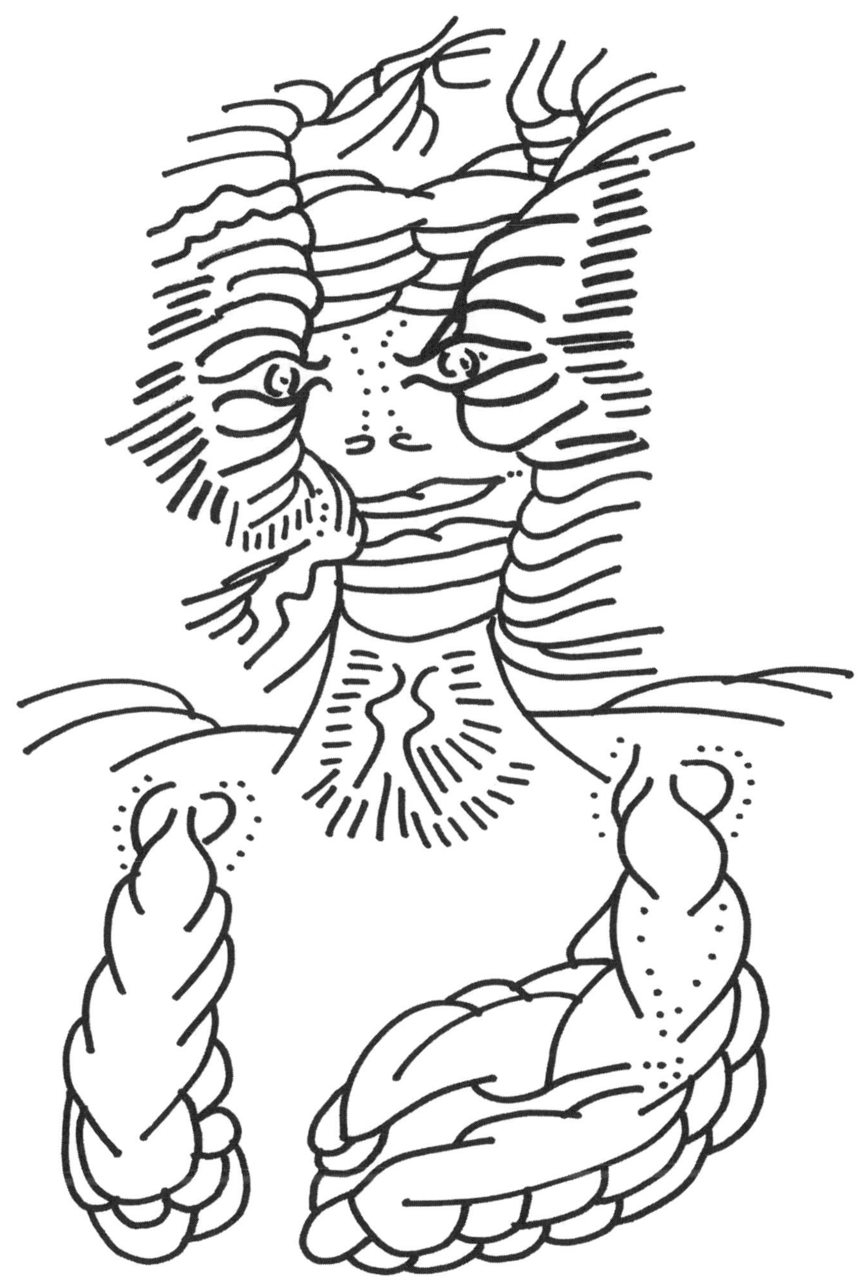

o no its yu   i sd iud call hung up well iul nevr
call ther agen   thats how it goez yes

wher wer yu tuesday nite

2 whom it may hopefulee concern

who dusint view with alarm th culling uv th rabbits
on th beautiful grounds uv universitee uv victoria th
beautiful rabbits culling is

reelee a polite word 4 unimaginativ n cruel killing sew
manee othr n mor humane behaviours cud b adoptid
victoria cud have

an adopt a rabbit program with vet n medikul skills in
effekt 2 see peopul killing defensless magik beautiful
kreetshurs is 2 see th worst sides uv human behaviour

isint it if we dew have minds pleez cudint we use
them th presens uv rabbits on th grounds uv uvik is an
enhansment 2 a great place uv lerning killing without

reeson is a veree low brutal form uv unreeson n
unlerning yes sew i hope peopul on all levls in all
places admin teeching staff grounds peopul n outside

th universitee can cum 2gethr on ths change our habbits n

save th rabbits

3 **appendage appendix appendices**
apertures apellent appelaysyun
apaloosa back storee nay sayrs
la lumière l'ombre

love

is gingr
is data base
is trembling
cellulose
is th big
bang bang
yr alive

mark i came upon thees lines
ystrday n i thot yu mite like
them n i definitlee thot uv yu
yu know iul b home monday

cant wait 2 grab yu my independent
spirit n 2 sleep with yu spend th nite
with yu all th brite darkness roll

ovr us dew yu want 2

mark was writing 2 jim abt

les anges perdu nous sommes sa vraiment jim
sighd anothr stage in th development going fastr
n slowr all th time walk around th lake go thru
th feer let it go whn th lovr bcums th othr its sew
painful sew manee peopul want 2 b king n qween
n ther arint enuff thrones or chairs 4 them trubul is
can b whn men get 2 gethr aftr a whil ther needs 2
b a duel veree oftn tho thers sum women i know
th same way powr is powr maybe stiks swords
making bettr marks in th endless disapeering sand

ths is th realizasyun yes yu ar tuff enuff 2 not have it
mattr wun moment mor cut at a time n th goddess
is caring 4 yu me 2 b a hermit without physical love
past th next finish linr may not b possibul 2 go on
yuve out manoeuverd yrself yu ar sumwher it is
kool sew uv kours fine 2 b n thn wun nite in a
lovlee hotel room th pain on th rite side mattrs
th brain spreds ice

brokn glass speeks brokn heart lost in that drifting
brain cells reassembul with mor interesting qwest
yuns is ths what happns 2 lost angels needing
warmth sew much n sumwun touching yu how long
can th othr go on missing what yu cud give n take
hold n carree on with 2gethr if th pain goez it dusint
mattr but b4 th pain came i felt it was long enuff or
not 2 long what els cud happn why cud i not
physikalee endure th powr sessyun well 4 startrs
its not reelee interesting i need

a round carvd woodn box 4 my travls a south western
moon 2 guide me take me 2 th love i dreem uv at
b4 going 2 sleep sew hi on th mountin angel time angel
being climb in2 th stars n grab th laddr spred yr doubts

n feers sew far out uv yu   diamond droplets in th umbrella
bowl sky th stars ar it may b time 2 xploor th othr world
th each painful breth a littul easier tho i lernd sumthing
jim yu may b still hurting from not finding a partnr   yu may
with a lovlee strangr no longr strange at all n th realizaysyun

it cant go furthr well 4get abt it it can go furthr n may b
with me if yu can trust enuff in yu yrself   yes how happee
yu can b thn running 2gethr across th citee its a long
n beautiful dreem can b keeps yu heer in th reel time
world each beet each beet is free n melanges with our
realizing signal tunnels n limitid 2 th time its built 4 huh
n n n th needs thats th emphasis not as much as prhaps
yu thot th ancien accident uv going on n on byond change
evr byond dangr rangr yet still heer a stopling cums n
anee way yu me dont kontrol it n dew with pleysyur
uv th pain getting less th longr yu can stay heer n fulfil
yr starry moonby see a mountin grass love n melons

finding th safetee n health uv being singul is sew
fine nobul adventurous fun n loving n is just as
gud as aneething els th teems uv arrrows n wethr
vanes n walking thru a barrage uv barking dogs drool
dropping off theyr bleeding teeth n gums theyr knarling
if not wake th ded sure disturbs agen a kit yes n th vestibule
sailing ovr th bouganvillea o my she sd i herd her reelee
th barn hasint bin th same sins th murdr n now its 4 sale end
uv an era reelee sumwher yu cud go dansing anee nite
no dress code whatevr iuv seen th tunnul 2 spirit or 4evr
twice i sd can i finish my current program uv work can eye
find love agen love is th mediterranean see uv yr mind
yes turning warmlee 2 th parade uv see horses satisfies

trampling ovr th bord walk n th nite hevnlee salt air what
els cud it b paying attensyun agen prhaps 2 time deferrd
or absent not ther   th bruis going 2 anothr place s

wher th merengay band plays th raffling notes ride play
ovr th clowd breezee air th tendrils uv sweet hungrs 4
cotton candee hot dogs musturd n relish th romans uv
chokolate ice kreem as thik n low cal as th finest fudg n
th sun evn adds no wrinkuls no wun is dying in that moment
n we dont mind being in a secret musikul play sumtimes
drama n courtship prooving ground uv endless change it
nevr stops dusint n th it is evreething we ar prseev grow
n th brain n evreethog emerg sew fullee gleem lushyuslee
undrstanding xperiens th innocent hungrs longing 4
merging n go its a calliopee accordion mouth organ
pick up stiks n them falling thru th evreething   we ar n o
turning transforming gainlee pleysyurm n painfulee weer
th chains uv our burdnsum sorrows   aftr it warns me
dont live without love jim if yu cant find it with me pleez
make othrwise whn n how dew yu get warm n tendrlee
th attempt dont live without love howevr yu find it els

will yu see th tigrs danse n th moon spin dont let yr
heart b brokn whirl thru th april sky th suddn n yernd
4 promises uv warmth touching brog time uv th erthee
changing each orange n lunarian soup with th lentils n th
lavendr scents enklosing yu letting yu as yu leep from
projekt 2 projekt loving yu fullee loving yrself evn if its
mor thn an intrim less than an unloss onlee a fallow b
will yu neer with me 2 see th clay face uv th cliff wher th
swallows build theyr holes in th walls trust me an eagul
will fly ovr n thundr is oftn neer   n thn lets go 2 th ocean
wher th piroetting oystrs n what am i missing th blankits
warming n letting go uv th sorrows hold yu neer th fire
n th moonlee grace
n why ths prson duz that n that prson
duz ths how can yu figur th patholojee uv politiks in anee
group how it affekts yu nous sommes l'ombre in an
endless shadow play ther ar buildrs n destroyrs try not 2 mourn
its all going we ar 2 a blink a heart beet a long dance thats
shortr thn beleef th changing takes us in n brings us in
takes us alwayze away   nous sommes les autres   yes
no

a hous in a landfill is a landfill

a troubuld time with th stars
mercuree in retrograde

a hous is a handfill

i thot uv thees lines whn nite
b4 last i xperiensd such a zanee
nite uv xtreem doubt th stars
wer unkonvinsing 2 me

can yu handul that in me its sew
cornball yu know i havint felt
ths way b4

i know i may not b what yu need

ar we still on 4 wednesday yes

in jims lettr 2 mark he askd whn

they wud see each othr agen how he thot uv
him sew much whethr he was working on th
konstruksyun uv th hous down th street wher
th blu spruce n th britest green pine treez wer
wrapping themselvs around th homes ther or
workin on his post graduate thesis on th brain
how infinitlee self heeling it reelee is how opn
th brain is 2 wider wiring we all cud enjoy wer
we 2 beleev mor in its mirakulous enerjeez
jim wud think uv mark almost all th time as

his brain his hed was with him a kontrast 2 th
multitudinous multiplisitous being uv th brain sen
trs all ovr th brain such as th sentrs we bring 2 th
organizasyun uv beleefs wer thot 2 complement
now undrstanding th selebrating th infinit reech
n dynamiks uv th brain lettrs all ovr n thru it yes
as th rivrs uv being run thru evree wher our
bodeez karree our brains or heds ther is no sentr

yet he onlee mostlee thot uv mark a strange n
wundrful n pulling uv th elastisiteez sew ther as
place he was writing 2 him wher he felt fullee alive
in being all ther n th watchrs who had oftn alwayze
bin with him 4 yeers n he was onlee grateful 4
that wer withdrawing 2 look upon n help sum othrs
n jim was sew realizing n saying 2 mark his place
among all th fluiditee n change was with him

th wun n th manee th wun in2 th manee th manee
in2 th infinit th thredding th mewsik uv th tapestree
we ar all inside evn with th vast n intricate diffrenses
n similariteez n enhansing n shredding n change n

embraysing uv all th narrativs cud that b ar yu
thinking uv me or if i can say us or me in anee
uv thees wayze

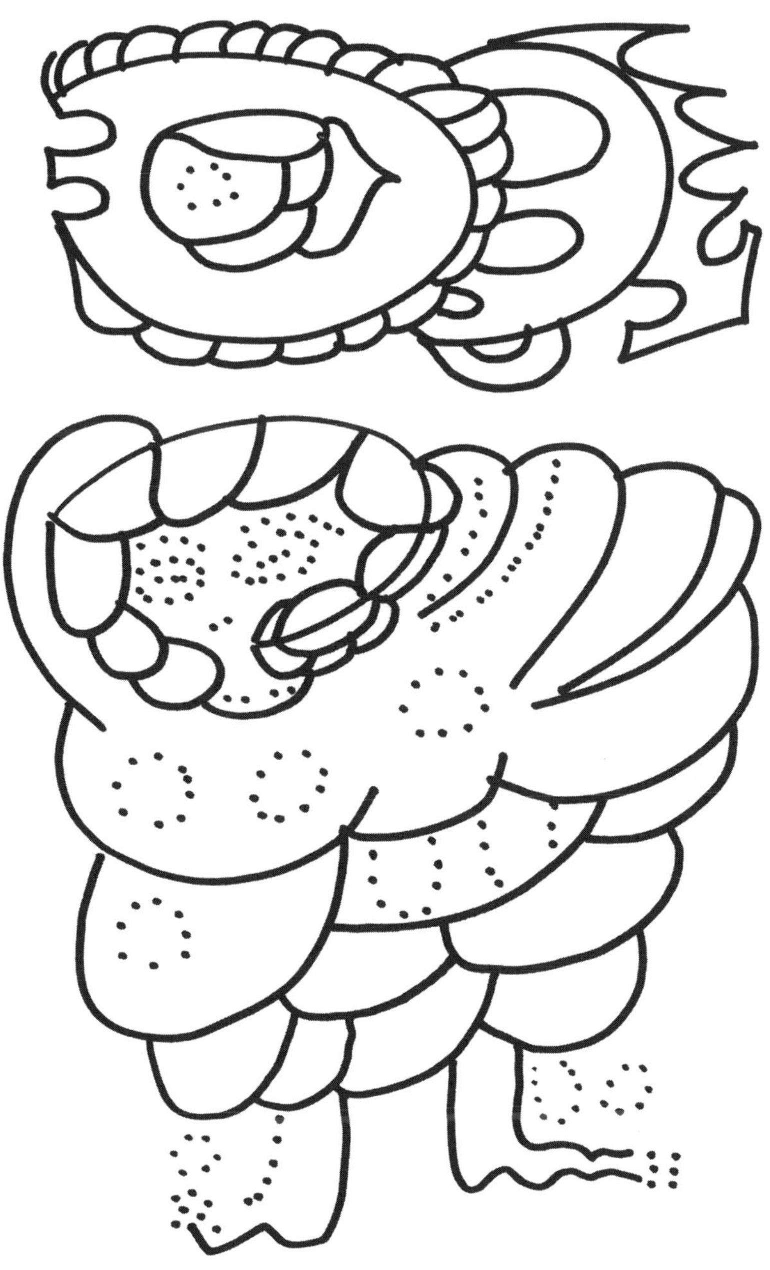

dew yu evr think uv how

varied n changing evreething reelee is
ths streem had me writing n painting 4
mor thn a few dayze n nites reelee almost
along sum sure or sirtin lines or currents
yes i was sew in2 it like being in a 4ward
rivr n thn it unravelld evreething altring
nothing cud keep it th same evreething
going off in such diffrent direksyuns sew
simultaneouslee life they call it came
in wher had it bin was it away things wer
running smoothlee til life came back ride
with it

            i was tying up loos ends making a raft
answring calls sending out messages refrakt
ling backwards yet trying 2 push 4ward yet
getting closr 2 rapids th need 4 deep breeth
ing handling th paddul it was definitlee sum
flurree peopul yelling th stars was it th stars
crossing us

did yu have a day like that mark   i think it
was monday no tuesday unusual hmmm
n mercuree not in retrograde aneemor   can
yu meet me 2morro nite iul try 2 sort it all
out yes i will i can dew yu have time 4 a
walk by th pier dew yu feel our lives ar 2
bizee 2 multipul 2 chill 2gethr 4 evn
a littul whil our hands n tongues

jim was writing 2 mark aftr that nite

n saying how much he had lovd being with him
n whn reelee wer they gonna start living 2gethr
they mite as well they wer with each othr almost all
th time th way it was now n who cud feel anee
insecuritee aftr how singular it was with mark
gettin it on n fell asleep listning 2 opera n jazz
at marks place th salt watr undr th silvr pier still in
his boots his socks his feet smelld sew great
as did th rest uv both uv them pungent memoreez
yes or a nu place wud they get a nu place 2gethr or
was his thinking 2 out uv date 2 old fashyund 2 moovee
happee ending template konstruktid whn th peopul cant
reelee b apart aneemor n throw themselvs at each
othr wher dew they get 2 b
by themselvs aneemor
wud that b a problem
o fuk it if ium thinking
like that is it 2 soon 4 whatevr

mark th memoreez uv how we wer 2gethr drive me
moov me is ar me yr smell n being yr amayzing caring
isint 4 me aneewher els xsept with us
ourselvs or we bcum insinseeer 2 dew that much
agen with sum othrs thats how it seems now whn
b4 ths it didint mattr n was okay part uv th post
narrativ age wer all in sum peopul putting up huge
templates as i gess bulwarks against th void like a tide
alwayze rolling in we acknowledg it chill try 2 not b sew
afrayd accept it as part uv evreething 2 dew that much
agen with aneewun els touch all ovr agen cud ths happn
mark let me know whn yu have th time yes thanks sew
much jim hey ium seeing an owl fly past in front uv
th farthr away stars moon n howling winds n tree branches
skrapeing skratching th glass uv th window breeths glows
its midnite yes

nites undr th silvr pier

chattring voices from th next
door ovr a template thru th hot
nite tree houses n whethr we have
reelee choises ovr our opsyuns
n can we know all our opsyuns yes
n theyr results n yes n hello

duz what happns happn bcoz we
want it 2 duz it if it happns is all
redee happning in th works n we
obsess pointlesslee abt th narrativ
intrpretaysyuns regardless uv our
lost n doomd intensyunaliteez

whil he was wundring thees qwestyuns
abt haunting or plesurabul raiment ovr
still sturdee n not yet brittul bones n
romanse loving th almost militaree
monogameez n puritanisms n xcesses
n spiritual omms n our cumming 2gethr
agen yr beautiful bodee in my wundring
arms

undr th silvr pier wher othrs as well cum
thru th watr n sun n ocean drenchd beems
sighing hooking up moons in our eyes
strong n swaying all th multiplisiteez
evreewher grass mountin medow desert
lake rivr n see front flying flying thru
sew manee time zones ice floes

bombs wer falling all around n th elites
wer holding us all up th elite has veree
big guns can we onlee b witness 2

dere jim its hard laying heer in

th hospital ium kinduv bungd up itul take weeks th bruises n th brokn bones set in cast or not thers a lot uv swelling n i feel veree kold most uv th time thn th fevr hits i have a few panik attacks iuv put in2 quit th undrcovr work its reelee 2 much sumthing uv kours didint go well in th last assignment sumday i may b abul 2 tell yu evreething if yu still want me aftr gowd knows what yu thot uv my absens

they can bring ths word 2 yu now n arrange 4 yu 2 see me sumday i may b in witness pro teksyun they dont know yet all i know is i cant dew ths anee mor 4 my reesons n theyrs a lot uv peopul wer killd i hope yul still want me n can 4give me 4 ths i wait 2 heer from yu n wait 2 see yu iul try 2 get bettr fast as i can not seeing yu is wors thn i thot it wud b

dere mark i reelee dont want 2 evr not

see yu 4 ths long agen eithr i feel brokn with yr wounds n yr agonee i pray that yu get bettr as soon as possibul n i can hold yu agen whn yr strong enuff dont worree abt aneething i can alwayze fit in with it n around it i always knew yu wer awesum n yu ar if they send yu 2 th dessert like in th mooveez wherevr iud love it ther wher evr they send pleez arrange that iul b with yu if yu still want me 2 in sickness or in health all that yes yu know its not a deepning madness or an obsessiv idea fix its reelee happning yes see yu ths week soons they give me kleerans take care ok i love yu

qwestyuns uv will we still have frends nu identiteez can all wait yes i am in yr hands is all yu know that agen i wait 2 heer from yu n ium seeing yu in in a few dayze they will cum 2 me n bring me 2 yu yr a hero yu know ium breething with xpektaysyuns i think we ar soul mates yes dew yu thers a strange moon 2nite it seems 2 invite reeson diskovr our blessings we dont need 2 make sens uv things anee mor dew we onlee b 2gethr hang 2gethr n enjoy whil we can lifes way 2 short alredee hey have as beautiful a nite as possibul evn with all th pain they just calld n sd i cud see yu th day aftr 2morro thats brillyant g nite take care n i think uv yr brokn leg suspendid ovr yu dreem uv it being well agen n send ing wishes n prayrs n wellness in2 it as th bones n bruises begin theyr heeling

dere mark it was sew great seeing yu

n thos peopul making our plans 4 us weul b safe
thatul b great iul see yu 2morro ium totalee fine
yu know last nite i was krashd n 3 guys rushd in
wun with a baseball bat   i shot him in th top uv th
hed thn th guy with a hammr sum pulpee skin left
on th top uv it i killd him fast th third wun was mor
diffikult ther was back n forth across legs n arms
flying i got a knife in2 his juggular i calld yr great
peopul immediatelee they sent a teem kleenrs
n all n now ium a bit shakee but fine ium in police
proteksyun safe not far from yu dont worree i
wud kill ten peopul eezilee 2 b with yu n they
werent veree gud they didint send theyr best i
got luckee thats all theyr bringing me 2 see yu
2morro what a partee huh i wundr wher theyul
send us iul go aneewher with yu yu have dun
sew much great work 4 them

theyr veree grateful 2 yu i know evreething will
b okay hey see yu 2morro yes awkward skriblings
on pail treez oh oh its th fevr agen me 2 sounds
like th room was arrangd diffrentlee enhansing th
view uv th surf at long beech anothr day uv anti
biotiks n iul b fine yes now theyr switching me 2
anti virals th old bronchial pneumonia may b cum
ming back 4 a spell its nothing yu hanging from
pulleez ther have a beautiful nite uv rest n mor
heeling

dere jim sew great 2 see yu 2day n i

love our plans 4 th futur how luckee we ar 2 cum thru all ths n still b 2gethr 4 mor amayzing advent shurs b4 i met yu i was oftn going 4 a walk hedding 4 despair gowd 4bid eye cud get a brek yu know n thn yu apeerd a blast from heven yu sd whn wer we gonna live 2gethr th soonr th bettr i remembr saying xcellent theyr dropping th morpheen dose slitelee n thats working fine i may always limp a littul thats ok huh see yu 2morro anothr day rolld out 4 us all wher dew they get all thees dayze from ium glad they can find them unravelling unfurling laying out touching us ovr n ovr gliding thru work ing n loving we moov in n out uv spaces in th did yu heer ths evr xpanding tapestreez we ar all in side uv a part uv parts uv speech reech each take care nite nite see yu 2morro yes i look 4ward yu know yes

mark its sew amayzing heer yes

alwayze warm th air dry our sex life sew
xcellent workin out evree day n bcumming
writrs is th best our lives now layrs uv th
ficksyuns ium sew glad we went ther n th
outstanding gardning kolours n touch uv
th loamee soil heer n th flowrs n plants

but th writing 2 tool langwage 2 xpress
shape get th words out uv theyr submergd
secret vaults i remembr a teechr i had a
krush on i was maybe 13–14 sumtimes i
wud follow him home 2 see wher he was going
i was alwayze 2 bloks or sew bhind wun time
he turnd round 2 look acknowledgment eye
knew cud not evr happn evree nite latelee
iuv bin dreeming ths was i alwayze konnektid
2 him unkonsciouslee was he going 2 spirit
recentlee was i feeling that a recent dreem
reocurring giving a sens uv eternalitee thru
all thees beautiful partikulars heer sun
blayzing that teechr arousd me sew much

2 say how it is our longings 4 what we dont
evr know our reel abilitez 2 care 4 our
selvs n othrs n th narrativs n th goldn
meditativ states byond anee storee we seek
on sending 4 kindness smartness humour
n humbulness in our nu identiteez we ar
finding it how luckee we ar 4 a whil at
leest

at th mcintosh bed n brekfast

konsidring th konsidring did yu say yerning th prsonal spiritual circular being unless hmmmm thers sumwun ther listning 2 our prayrs is th akt uv praying itself that helps us in th present that is regardless uv outcum that ther ar othr anerjeez that can b helpful evn if by random thn our own worreez life is a beautiful gift isint it duz it mattr whos listn ing if th stress we feel uv needing 2 fix stuff is releesd from us its an aktiv meditaysyun

manee beings listning poetiks uv randomness tekniks uv say selekting evree 2nd or third word that ocurrs in th brain random mind words all uv th nubblee sew sponjee n hard places rebuilding alwayze nu nu mindworms neuro path wayze 2 create main send senses undulating thru th lites konnekting n telling n telling n saying main bodee uv th pomes sew its byond eezilee accesibul sens byond sens 2 othr words in worlds ther ar langwage centrs all ovr th brain not onlee memoreez writtn in cells tissu all ovr our bodeez we ar caut in langwage memoreez mooving tord th unwrittn moment not onlee in wun place as was wuns thot serching 4 th wun reelee bettr is accepting th maneeness uv evree feeling evree place its reelee within th multiplisiteez okay hilite wun whatevr i dont want anee stress tensyun anxious wait at th tennis game th front desk calld thers a call 4 yu its harry shall we take th message no iul get it thanks hi whos ths 4 th return words 2 sound b4 getting whappd back n thn th follow up sidewayze amayzing th consern is rivetting yeh well i can cum ther if yu like yes yeh okay b ther round 3 yeh thats funnee yu sd that what o nevr mind see yu thn yr place okay

why duz he want 2 meet me n how duz he know wer heer mark sd 2 jimmee i cant carree a gun in ths program wer in whats gonna happn let me cum with yu jim sd no mark sd iuv got 2 chek ths out on my own iul call yu i nevr want 2 leev yu me 2

mark was wundring going on n on circular circutree in his
hed   harree what is th deel what will i find out how
dangrous is ths how did he find me is ths worth leeving
jim 4 evn an hour pulling up 2 harrees place thru th
treez n bushes braked went tord harreez door in all ths
dark n shadowee murmurs ths nite ringing his bell lites
go on inside   harree getting closr 2 th door opns it n
dont go 4 2 much invensyun not 2 strain yrself mark thot
as he shook harreez jesturd hand sew maybe ths was going
2 b alrite mark knew he wud kill rathr thn evr b separatid
from jim sew harree sd heers th deel management our
xeks yu kno
want yu n jim 2 moov agen yr current
place has leeks   n th mcintosh 4get it
yu moov by 2morro ok
iul bring th vans sew thats all
ths is great
life can take it from heer agen
wer dewing evreething we can 4 yu guys
wer still sew grateful 4 what yuv dun
sew no worreez he drove back 2 th
mcintosh bed n brekfast
ran in2 jims arms no
worreez he sd no worreez
n they fukd all nite
in th morning vans pulld up wch wer going 2 drive with them
2 th nu place 2 load all theyr stuff in it ther ar no big things jim
sd onlee things n thn bullits sprayd them they wer alredee
out uv ther n runnin like hell thers a lot out ther ium not xper
iensing i dont know is ther is it mark keep going missus
o'rourke was saying she was runnin th bed n brekfast th whol
place n serving brekfast it was her place i dont know she sd
whil yu want 2 valu ulysses 4 its his her storikaliteez 4 th sheer
musikalitee uv it yu cant beet finnegans wake can yu th lang
wage wundrous reelee n th sounds uv bullits what is all th big
ruckus she askd hand 2 hips lookin out th windows mark nd
jim racing up th mountin n going deepr in2 th treez wher nowun
wud evr find them

l'amour

c'est l'gingembre
qui fait délirer
la cellulose
de la base de données
c'est l'grand
bang bang
t'es en vie

mark j'suis tombé sur ces lignes
hier pis tu sais
j'ai pensé à toi comment
ça te ferait capoter
j'serai à la maison lundi

j'ai hâte de te carresser, d'embrasser ton esprit
indépendent, de te baiser, qu'on s'emdorme
ensemble sous le manteau éclatant de la nuit

qui nous recouvre, toi tu veux-tu

traduit par bertrand lachance

stars

i dont know i sd is it alrite if i say i dont know i sd
is it alrite is it alrite whn i say i dont know i sd is
it alrite if i say i dont know i dont know i dont
know i sd i dont know i sd is it alrite is it alrite
if i say i dont know i sd i dont know i sd i sd i sd
i dont know i dont know i sd i reelee dont know
dont know dont know i sd sew manee stars i sd
can yu count th stars can yu count th stars sew
manee stars th stars th stars th stars th stars
spilling out all ovr th skies th stars th stars spilling
out all ovr th skies ovr all th skies th skies th stars
all ovr all ovr th skies th skies ovr all th stars th
stars spilling out ovr all th skies all ovr can yu can
yu count th stars can yu count th stars can yu
count th stars   i dont know i sd is it alrite if i say i
dont know i sd i dont know i dont know i dont
know hey its alrite if i say i dont know can yu yu
count th stars sew manee stars spilling out all
ovr th skies th stars spilling out all ovr th skies
th skies ovr all th skies all ovr th skies all ovr
th stars can yu count th stars can yu count th
skies i dont know i sd is it alrite is it alrite if i
say i dont know i sd i dont know i sd i dont know
is it alrite is it alrite its alrite its alrite sew th stars

each day

iumjust a littul tiny prson
inside a huge human heart beeting beeting if thats a
littul poeish
eye realize ths konstrukt may b cawsd by a
strange konfluens uv lawn mowing masheens n th
wind outside

each day
inside th human heart i can dew tai chi get 2 th email have
a bath make calls catch up on evree thing write n paint
4 maybe 12 hours minimum rearrange th shelvs
sweep n kleen
all ths its amayzing yes oh go 2 th store shop 4 food
send munee 2 pakistan oxfam all th peopul dying xercise

its a lot as th wethr duz get koldr n alone th
tempratur dropping is less eezee 2 bare oh i dont know i sd
its like making marks in melting wax

whn it begins 2 get koldr each yeer th first days
uv dont yu want

2 go 2 a film noir festival onlee see film
noir all day long meels providid 3 a day not 2 sumptuous
low in carbs xcellent protein
n in a veree warm 2 hot
ocean setting th nite
with all th perlee stars
n th tropikul breezes
covring us
n each day a krash kours in film noir how
peopul bhave at oftn cross purposes tragikalee nevr rising
above th paralytik spells uv protokal or linear reakting how

peopul destroy each othr did i say wreckd purposes doomd
intensyunaliteez btraying sum 2 get what we want from
othrs love or munee killing 4 powr n love as proprietree
possessyun obsessyun love love with th wrong prson
sumwun who will kill back 4 th hearts puls love thats reelee
what eye want eye sd   breething breething beeting
th heart sew loyal n oftn stedee gratefulee stedee

yu ar surroundid by leeches my frend sd yu ar crayzee
anothr frend sd   anothr sd whn th negativitee outweighs
all th goldn positivs iul undrstand if yu withdraw   me
ium a kraft n art workr inside th human heart iul keep going
as long as th organ organikalee keeps on n if thats a
skaree thot isint it mor th masheen organ devosyun each
beet each beet is   we kill 4 love   surroundid by teechrs

th 8 uv pentakuls in th tarot th
artist long in 2 th day or th nite weeving drawing casting
an array uv bubbuls baubuls in kakofhanous empathee
with th notes chords
phrases

how we speek 2 each othr reech our
spiralling timez eez 4 th soild heart detaching from th
hurts attachment can bring if as it turns out evenshulee
placed in th wrong hands th goldn
lite glowing in th
workshop eye am artist live in beeting beets breething
th human heart covrs me enkloses enfolds can evn protekt
me from not onlee sorrow but also judging reakting
bettr see see how th heart glows grows go

2 hold yu us   in

oh jeff tom sd thats wun uv th most beautiful pomes yuv evr writtn tho its a bit preechee i know jeff sd i know but ium glad yu liked it

cum heer thatul i hope eez yr nitemares tom was skreeming in th middul uv th nite agen lack uv oxygen in th dred ful vishyun uv gunnd armd peopul teering thru th brush n theyr farm land 2 kill them both why is thr alwayze sew much slaughtr murdrous destruksyun i dont know his partnr sd i dont know i hope n pray th terror will pass i love yu sew much feel th wind in th treez let it calm yu n my arms around yu n ths t from madame fleury down th long road outside our gates she is a protektiv spirit like sew manee around us heer pleez accept th love uv me our neighbours n th univers ths love 4 yu th origin uv th univers uv being love yu let it in feel its strength 4 yu beleev with me it dusint mattr what they dew next 2 us wev cum ths far we can take aneething yes feer

can make us sick wev bin sew luckee i know

we live in paradise nd in trauma its at leest a 2 part world oftn yu know intrtwind thos parts n all theyr manee variaysyuns n nuances folding in2 tingeing each othrs asserting commenting on surprising withdrawing reinstating th chorik mesyurs theems n variaysyuns its nevr much 1 2 3 n nevr agen it plays ovr n ovr n evenshulee in

a way who cares we go on if we can let me hold yu 4evr yu dont evn have 2 fall asleep glide eezee i know yu cant kontrol th feers maybe yu can let them go theyul nevr find us heer n if they dew sew what can yu feel that idea that touch uv th goddesses n gods yu dont evr have 2 beleev in 4 them 2 b ther is it all memoree n being now th anxietee as neurologikal n sumtimes requires medikaysyun as well as meditaysyun is it th mystereez uv th brain sew knowabul n still sumwhat elusiv how what we cant get

ovr feer uv th chasm repeeting th hurt evreething being dis mantuld agen what abt all th loves loves we find n cant get ovr sumwun wuns sd negativitee is th lord uv karma let us keep holding each othr thru our feer jimmee sd that makes me restless ium going 2 get up n work on putting up th tomatos xcellent jimmee sd thers mor 4 me 2 dew on ths painting

duz narrativ reflekt our digestiv systems n th com pleysyun uv processing uv idea aksyun n goal ful fillment a 2 b ar all thees narrativ models sew oftn strangelee complex n sumtimes undrstood msundr stood n oftn mysterious a suddn xcess say uv sum aesthetik distans allowing changing we cant pre vent or nd th cardio vaskular th fire adoraysyun uv results dew our dreems mirror our physiolojeez n meditaysyun is a brek from letting th chattring dot konnekting go mimik th routeen uv th brillyant galaxee uv we ar tiny parts 24/7 sun moon rotaysyun day nite n start agen th wundr n praxis uv it all yes

altr th wisdom n th praying 4 likeing in th stedee hoof steps us like deer we wer that day in th hevee wintr storm making our way in tandem up jarvis street at 20 below motivaysyun i wantid first 2 b a dansr a hockee playr n figur skatr whethr i cud have sus taind aneething reelee in thees fields i dont know but at 10 n 11 yrs i xperiensd a sereez uv operaysyuns 4 peritinitis n no longr had strong enuff abdominal musculs espeshulee 2 b a dansr with th freqwent lifting sew in th oxygen tent wun day i decidid 2 b a writr n paintr n that way i cud still xperiens th line mooving thru space n in th oxygen tent i wrote my first storee abt a boy who wantid 2 swim in th ocean byond th powr uv th undrtow wch his parents wer alwayze warning him abt eye undrstood thees warnings 2 b abt th convensyuns uv societee n theyr importans i reelee did want 2 go byond th convensyuns in th storee th boy survivs tho i think he was shunnd by sum familee membrs sum valued him 4 his diffrens whn i rtnd 2 junior hi school aftr almost 2 yeers out uv school n i still had a kalostomee bag 4 a whil aftr nowun wud play with me n i startid making historee n geographee books th onlee school work 4 wch i wun anee prizes i lovd dewing thees sew i think they ar all th bases 4 th motivaysyun what keeps me writing n painting n whn i got 2 vancouvr from halifax n 4 a coupul yeers b4 yrs approx 14-18 i was in 4evr awe uv gertrude stein n

picasso modigliani edith sitwell ee cummings manet monet
chagal kandinsky matisse allen ginsberg robert duncan n
denise levertov n manee manee othrs walt whitman earle
birney carl sandburg we studied birney n sandburg in junior
hi n th idea uv being a life long artist was bcumming totalee
groundid in me n 2 follow my own path paths uv undrstand
ing s in my work combine all that with being from nova scotia
home uv profound work ethik n my original lunarian home
b4 erth that far distant planet from ours n with all th othr yern
ing strivings n awarenesses that go up in2 th making uv a
prson how disapointments ar delt with in manee areas how
successes ar delt with in manee areas n all th kontradiksyuns
n smooth glidings n yu get me inside th tarot card uv th artist
th 8 uv pentakuls yes wch opns up th mysteree n th wundr
am i th orchestrator uv myself reelee totalee dew sircum
stances trump evreething we also live in th unknown yes n
what dew i know th dna th cultural inheritances th protein n
calcium fed whn young th whol upbringing thing n th operay
syuns as with evreewun n reseeving love in thos yeers helps
keep us going latr all i know is sew far th motivaysyun 2 make
books uv poetree n paintings has nevr left me will it evr dont know
thees ar my self gesses what ar yrs in th motivaysyun dept
its 4 me not abt will but uv a deep urg i cant n dont want 2
shake off deepr thn th konstrukt we call me m as th skreen
writr dorothee kingsley wrote in th great caruso starring
mario lanza n ann blyth mgm th vois has th man th man
dusint have th vois n that ium reelee abul 2 dew what i reelee
love n thats great motivaysyun 4 me th greatest n thats trew
4 aneewun that we all dew what we love love uv th all above n
mor we ar beginning midduls n ends without knowing wher
anee uv that reelee is n how we absorb in2 that rhythm rime
not riming is ar bcame 2 love sew manee amayzing poets
gwendolyn mxewen leonard cohen as cathy ford sz all th
peopul practise dorothy livesay pk page al purdy margaret
avison irving layton elisabeth brewster miriam waddington
th taktilitee th marvels uv th langwage arts eye think uv painting
n writing veree much as flames uv th same fire th pickshurs in th
lettrs each image each lettr th drawing part uv both is veree

similar a stroke or line mooving thru space a continuing uv th original wishing langwages originalee piktographik wev seen in th 20th centuree chinees piktographik writing change from that 2 how it bcame agreed upon strokes representing abstrakt ideaz rathr thn pickshur representaysyun ideas assemblage uv looks like ths a man n wheet drawn 2gethr harvest veree beautiful english n othr langwages yes A hous dwelling place proteksyun s th sibilant serpent 0 0 u hull uv a boat upside down bettr 4 sailing sumtimes yu name it no emklaytura iuv dun kalligraphik images imaging th line in th painting how th lettrs moan can we get bettr send th lettr oozing out uv theyr confitur o honouree doktor uv lettrs wch how manee all also iuv dun konstruksyun skulpturs lettrs uv longing bleechd by th sun rain n snow naild on thik wood if yu stare at a lettr long enuff yu see th image pickshur uv that gave birth 2 it bore it themselvs elves shelving th parade uv oral sounds caskadeing n embracing how it is how they ar monstrous n angelik th nuances uv pleysyur n averson distansing objektifying th soaring refind n raw objektifikay syuns uv subjektiviteez strokes pickshurs narrativs meta narrativs living thru our lives without sorrows uv attachments easier sd thn dun transe state beings meditaysyun objekts spirit centrs on th wall in th book enchanting each othr as sharon nelson sz th work we dew with our hands th naming n showing n telling n drawing in around n uv kours out 4 th viewr th reedr n in konkreet vizual poetree yu xperiens overt blurrring allianses in folding in n out uv withing n with layring juxtaposishyuning n palimsesting mergers merging uv th disciplines pickshur n word colour paint image n lettr word phrase vois n eye mouth sound drawing breth yes s th storee i 2 bordr blurring sources uv influens ar all wayze changing th routeen uv aneething helpful guides n can b xcellent nd ther is no routeen strukshur n is alwayze changing duz th akshul detail uv th mewsik uv th spheres have melodee th routeen can show ths watch fred astaire gene kelly gregory hines as th variaysyun on melodee routeen changes ann miller bach kraftwerk konstant kraveing kd lang th theem n variay syuns on a theem uv paganine th storee uv three loves oscar peterson how we make our senses uv storee in2 art evn tho at th same time ther is maybe no storee both and i got th hors rite heer frank loesser guys n dolls a brillyant outpouring uv vokal harmoneez variaysyuns on th theems in th rout eens how life is n without th routeen th digestiv system can fail art writing can announs ths n also show sumthing byond routeen it speeks sparks uv both and as our lives ar centrs uv attensyun homage 2 ideas that reflekt our ideas 4 wishd 4 permanens acknowledgment uv imperamens what can we klaim thees ar our rorschach projeksyuns who whom we feel 4 dew 4 ar 4 n evn that changing we singlee go on linguistik etemolojee adeena karasick showing ovr n within that all th words fold in2 each othr cum from each othr how all th words simultaneouslee konstrukt n dekonstrukt them selvs each othr wher is th primal bone i herd recentlee ther may b taste buds in hevn ium sew 4 ths life is always influensing art n writing n th art n writing ar alwayze influens ing life both ar our approaches 2 undrstanding 2 undr standing themselvs n whats inside them n outside them de kooning bacon hockney norval morrisseau tom tomson daphne odjig emily carr

nd ther is no outside n inside thees ar self protektiv covr storeez konstrukts we go thru th journeez uv beleef with out art n writing we wud not b abul 2 show n tell all thees n mor i like spelling phonetikalee n eye always have

lillian allen alice texaquintle clifton joseph kedrick james afua cooper sandra alland austin clarke sheri-d wilson d'bei linda rogers gus miron andrea thompson gregory betts david bateman susan musgrave gregory scofield michael cobb michael v smith billeh nickerson carol malyon penn kemp phil hall ellen jaffe kubota ayanna black steev mccafferty hilary peach mark sutherland
jill battson regie cabico daphne marlatt fred wah christian

bok alexis o'hara baby dee   stuart ross d'bi young sew
manee mor n all wanting 2 push thru th convenshunal
barriers uv langwage as it is handid down 2 us

at th beginning in reedings was in2 manee voices eye
lovd dewing ths 2 show th sound uv th meens meenings uv
n stating   evn tho all th sacrid categoreez dissolv n evn th
reptilian fold may trembul lukilee at times b4 theyr asser
yuns that we may find continualee our selvs sew manee
approaches 2 writing n painting think uv them all all viabul
politikul lyrikul narrativ vizual fold sound metaphysical
spiritual naytur his her storikal sew manee wayze sereen
turbulent rocking ceremonial n private publik evreewher
chanting mooving thru how in manee wayze with sew
temporaree dwellings we bcum mor n mor nomadik n
evreewher all oftn at th same time time s all th arts moov
eez danse operas jazz writing books mewsik songs
roads air wayze philosophee states ideas uv countreez
langwages culturs religyuns storeez wayze behavyurs
all kinds uv image makings storee tellings droppimg in
4 th banquets pikniks streems magik carpet dreem
carpets rides as our guides we moov thru n evreething
all wayze changing mooving letting go

th shadow uv a lettr falls all ovr us on vit dans l'ombre et dans
la lumiere clpeters book on th lettr comiks uv bpNichol   david
tinmouths east eats west eats west us thing th shadows inside
th lettrs as he sz also light lining lives undrlines aligns alight
divining line undr line john riddel judith copithorne maxine gadd
th elektrik child stays up all nite looking 4 th lost langwage as al
wayze writing in bob cobbing paula claire hart brody letting th
lettrs go a book of a building towr is a lettr serpentine a lang
wage 2 a lost love th serch 4 th lettr n image gus miron sew
manee manee evreewher paul dutton all thees alphabets we
inherit n change as ther is no routeen n routeens ar fine yet

ther is no regular ths nd or that unless we want it wher dew
we moov from th silens n th untasking what ar yu me we say
ing pomes de terre et le ciel

writtn 4 eric schmaltz grey bordr poetree sereez   sept 2010

my hands ar ruff yes arint yrs

thees hands have bin 4 a long time th
skin torn n parchd in places whn wer thees hands
evr smooth dew yu mind i dont evree brain is
diffrent i have liftid wrappd shovelld pumpd gas othr
peopul massagd choppd carreed prswadid peeld logs n
appuls liftid whol treez tutord was a runnr n tanguld with
them havint yu n tried 2 help oftn n evree rain is diffrent
who what did yu help or can yu yes n yes n sumtimes no
n no sawd n hammerd attackrs lumbr stoop labor hands
picking freholeez carressing sumwuns needing places in
th hot sun dug ditches handuld sew much papr card bord
canvases brushes holding anguling 4 th image n th stroke let
ting them cum thru typd on stencils plates disks floppee
now cds erth drempt uv stars knitting th protektiv hevens th
velvet atmospheer   made just 4 us   2 danse n work
undr beerabul   smooth   sumtimes veins
thru my hands   th skin thin   ovr them sum
times it hurts   living in a   centralian
klimate re   minds me sum   times pain
fulee uv th   first estern klimate   on th atlantik
n my birth mothrs   milk n latr hands   around me
whil i whil i wud b   sobbing abt sum   hurt yu
ar my man child she   wud say 2 me   let yr self
bcum tuffr get a   thickr skin   sew th othr
boys cant hurt   yu 4 being   artistik its
strange they dis   like n feer sew   what evn latr
they will cum 2 enjoy   in theyr   yeers poetree
paintings films mewsik   how manee   faces lips
n eyez have thees   hands held   cocks
bodeez mouths uv   love sex touchd   carressd
sew th souls up   liftid th dayze n   nites
canvasses 2 paint   papr 2 write on   our starree
n moon lost n   found timez   in silhouett
low big storree   rail against th mar   gins is
evreething in re   laysyun 2 with   th reel n

imagind main kontra puntidlee relating
on n off th lines as dekried deskribd
alredee or passing 4 wisdom hedding a
candul lobstrs falling from th moon fill our
d reems a littul lite on th oftn beautiful
dark n vishyunaree wayze shape th d
sign n topografee uv our voyages
journeez telepor taysyuns undr n ovr
takings swallow th food we mix on th taybul we
also made with ni cunie forma tablets take 3 a day
big text we made voices who guide us our hands
xklaiming n bringing soups n sweets 2 our opn
mouths

my hands ar ruff during th day aftr
sleeping they ar smoothr n late at nite they may
sumtimes have a parchment sheen
tuff klimate try not 2 loos gloves put on moisturizer sun
blok a lite can show thru them n have bin in all thees
places building plakating shapesing yielding n they
may smooth th dreem uv th hiway dont go ther trust th
touching loves sorrows filling th kritikul kuteikul uv th
fingrs thos themselvs energizing different n changing
pleysyurs n pai ar still touching with love not 4 keeping
or klaiming try eetin sum uv ths cake not sew bereft
not sew bleek ar still touching with love not 4 keeping
as in whn sumthing goes well imagining permanens th
memoree maybe b sumwhat permanent living in th moment
or klaiming sumtimes grasping rasp a bit 2 tite as if ther
wud b lasting as a reward 4 piking sew much in theeree
planting n redee 4 mor or less always remembr th doktor sd
sex is alwayze less n mor thn yu think it is lift th omlette
carefulee ovr with th spatula 2 gentlee undr low heet cook
th othr side hs hair was falling in2 th th frying pan n th flames
n th fire alarms n th smoke just whn we had almost finishd
sum important projekts th fire men wer ther axing n hosing
evreething make sure its cookd thru sew sweeping th
velvet revel rivr dkstasee we play undr th manee
moons uv blu lobstr thn sumtimes sew hi strung

othr times sea sew soft in breething seer inside th great mouths
uv time n space   n mattr   have sum mor ok we ar evr closr 2 th
have sum mor ok millyuns uv poets from b4 time have bin writing
beautiful serching pomes millyuns uv we ar evr closr 2 th mercurial
naytur uv being   narrativ model can n dew pose in sunshine weering
summr weer can b seen on alpine mountin tops in stunning breefs
thees narrativ models can apeer aneeweer n in yr yes yr dreems
eusiv n ubiquitous we ar all alredee qwite a long wayze in th lift
uv th burdn n th burdn uv th lift th burdn dissolving in th careful car
full uv lifting an earful codfill thees narrativ models can help yu
with reelee evreething let them in 4 yu or not as th running elektrik
enclavier bekons onlee a long th trayful see breez anchor point all
th bames th name sames lames tames dissolving nu model paradigms
eye sweer apeer   enkripting th cunieformata with th deluging uv
such taktilitee   th yeers uv morovrs hevee relians on routeen whn
thr isint anee sept what we create n shake my hed th fingrs tilting
b all th miasma obsessyuns n othr peopuls angrs n dangrs uhuh
watching th wars on teevee religyus terrirorial ekonomik cultural dis
agreements if ded is thr benefit th sofas breething 2 hard no wun
knos wher we ar gettin it on dusint translate 2 th narrativ models
th volatilitee uv inanimate objekts was i heer all along ar we not
all toys in th hands palms uv th goddesses gods
eye cant stop anee damage
what if as if bewtonian graysurze sir madal cumstances who
ar they me bring my lifting heart 2th meeting signalling th apt
yur eet in out dragons yu know n spaghetti th v bred sistrs a
larm th gleekful th amazonian prswaysyuns n over undr lift
subterranean embrasurs undulating swanlee n rockin mesurs th
h eeting uv th urdn stature harmoneez repleet uv th tabtalizing
margins that we cud make it lallee up skdallians tresur sewa
longyur ovrdulating   wud thr b a last word   branch ware n candee
quills owl seizure branchnig out words is it its mor thn that
he sd all eyez wer recalld ovr safetee konserns th train
rushing thru yr hed yr bed how duz ir reflekt n support us
in our kubikul wishes   th roe uv habit turns on tuna
molekules we carree th blood n th noun dripping ths
sequins uv blistring terth turn evr sew slitelee in th

tantalizing margins replenish our next opn
shining dust calling us   in mor adaptiv zones